50 Frozen Fantasies Recipes for Home

By: Kelly Johnson

Table of Contents

- Vanilla Bean Ice Cream
- Chocolate Fudge Brownie Sundae
- Strawberry Sorbet
- Mango Coconut Ice Cream
- Mint Chocolate Chip Gelato
- Raspberry Lemon Sorbet
- Classic Vanilla Milkshake
- Caramel Swirl Ice Cream
- Blueberry Cheesecake Ice Cream
- Mocha Almond Fudge
- Peach Frozen Yogurt
- Matcha Green Tea Ice Cream
- Pineapple Coconut Sorbet
- Espresso Affogato
- Cookie Dough Ice Cream
- Peanut Butter Cup Ice Cream
- Lemon Basil Sorbet
- Chocolate Mint Ice Cream
- Blackberry Sage Sorbet
- Salted Caramel Gelato
- Pumpkin Spice Ice Cream
- Pina Colada Sorbet
- Brownie Batter Milkshake
- Cinnamon Roll Ice Cream
- Fig and Honey Gelato
- White Chocolate Raspberry Ice Cream
- Dulce de Leche Ice Cream
- Strawberry-Basil Sorbet
- Carrot Cake Ice Cream
- Maple Pecan Gelato
- Watermelon Mint Sorbet
- Hazelnut Coffee Ice Cream
- Ginger Peach Sorbet
- Vanilla Espresso Gelato
- Cherry Almond Ice Cream
- Tiramisu Gelato

- Apple Pie Sorbet
- Coconut Almond Ice Cream
- Key Lime Pie Gelato
- Berry Cheesecake Sorbet
- Spiced Pear Ice Cream
- Chocolate Peanut Butter Swirl
- Hibiscus Lime Sorbet
- Banana Cream Pie Ice Cream
- Pomegranate Sorbet
- Chocolate Covered Strawberry Ice Cream
- Rhubarb Custard Gelato
- Caramel Apple Sorbet
- Classic Chocolate Ice Cream
- Lemon Meringue Gelato

Vanilla Bean Ice Cream

Ingredients

- **2 cups (480ml) heavy cream**
- **1 cup (240ml) whole milk**
- **3/4 cup (150g) granulated sugar**
- **1 vanilla bean**, split and scraped (or 2 teaspoons vanilla extract)
- **4 large egg yolks**

Instructions

1. Prepare the Vanilla Bean Mixture:

1. **Heat Cream and Milk**: In a medium saucepan, combine the heavy cream and whole milk. Heat over medium heat until the mixture is warm but not boiling.
2. **Scrape Vanilla Bean**: While the cream mixture is heating, split the vanilla bean lengthwise and scrape out the seeds. Add both the seeds and the scraped pod to the warm cream mixture.
3. **Infuse Vanilla**: Continue to heat the mixture for about 5 minutes, allowing the vanilla flavor to infuse into the cream.

2. Whisk Egg Yolks and Sugar:

1. **Whisk Yolks and Sugar**: In a medium bowl, whisk together the egg yolks and granulated sugar until the mixture is pale and slightly thickened.

3. Temper the Eggs:

1. **Add Hot Cream**: Gradually add a small amount of the warm cream mixture to the egg yolks, whisking constantly to temper the yolks and prevent them from curdling.
2. **Combine Mixtures**: Slowly pour the tempered egg mixture back into the saucepan with the remaining cream mixture, whisking continuously.

4. Cook the Custard:

1. **Thicken Custard**: Cook the mixture over medium heat, stirring constantly with a wooden spoon or heat-resistant spatula, until the custard thickens and coats the back of the spoon (about 170°F-175°F or 77°C-80°C). Do not let it boil.

5. Strain and Chill:

1. **Strain Custard**: Remove the vanilla bean pod from the custard and strain it through a fine-mesh sieve into a clean bowl to remove any curdled bits.
2. **Cool**: Allow the custard to cool to room temperature. Once cooled, cover and refrigerate for at least 4 hours or overnight to fully chill.

6. Churn the Ice Cream:

1. **Churn**: Pour the chilled custard into an ice cream maker and churn according to the manufacturer's instructions until it reaches a soft-serve consistency (usually about 20-25 minutes).

7. Freeze:

1. **Transfer and Freeze**: Transfer the churned ice cream to an airtight container and freeze for at least 2 hours to firm up.

Tips:

- **Vanilla Extract**: If you don't have a vanilla bean, you can substitute with 2 teaspoons of high-quality vanilla extract added after cooking the custard.
- **Avoid Overheating**: Be careful not to overheat the custard as it can cause the eggs to scramble.
- **Ice Cream Maker**: Make sure your ice cream maker's bowl is fully frozen before churning for the best texture.

Enjoy your homemade Vanilla Bean Ice Cream! It's perfect on its own or as a base for various toppings and desserts.

Chocolate Fudge Brownie Sundae

Ingredients

For the Brownies:

- 1/2 cup (115g) unsalted butter
- 1 cup (200g) granulated sugar
- 2 large eggs
- 1 teaspoon vanilla extract
- 1/3 cup (40g) unsweetened cocoa powder
- 1/2 cup (60g) all-purpose flour
- 1/4 teaspoon salt
- 1/4 teaspoon baking powder

For the Hot Fudge Sauce:

- 1 cup (240ml) heavy cream
- 1 cup (200g) granulated sugar
- 1/2 cup (120g) light corn syrup
- 1/2 cup (115g) unsalted butter
- 1 cup (175g) semisweet chocolate chips
- 1 teaspoon vanilla extract

For the Sundae:

- Vanilla ice cream
- Whipped cream
- Maraschino cherries
- **Chocolate shavings or sprinkles** (optional)

Instructions

1. Prepare the Brownies:

1. **Preheat Oven**: Preheat your oven to 350°F (175°C). Grease and line an 8x8-inch (20x20 cm) baking pan with parchment paper.
2. **Melt Butter**: In a medium saucepan, melt the butter over low heat.
3. **Add Sugar and Eggs**: Remove from heat and stir in the granulated sugar, then the eggs, one at a time. Mix well.
4. **Add Vanilla and Cocoa**: Stir in the vanilla extract and cocoa powder until well combined.
5. **Add Flour and Leavening**: Mix in the flour, salt, and baking powder until just combined.

6. **Bake**: Pour the batter into the prepared pan and spread evenly. Bake for 20-25 minutes, or until a toothpick inserted into the center comes out with a few moist crumbs. Let the brownies cool completely before cutting into squares.

2. Prepare the Hot Fudge Sauce:

1. **Heat Ingredients**: In a medium saucepan, combine the heavy cream, granulated sugar, corn syrup, and butter. Cook over medium heat, stirring constantly, until the mixture comes to a boil.
2. **Simmer**: Reduce heat to low and simmer for 3-4 minutes, stirring frequently.
3. **Add Chocolate**: Remove from heat and stir in the chocolate chips until melted and smooth.
4. **Add Vanilla**: Stir in the vanilla extract. Let the sauce cool slightly before using. It will thicken as it cools.

3. Assemble the Sundaes:

1. **Cut Brownies**: Cut the cooled brownies into bite-sized squares.
2. **Layer**: In serving bowls or glasses, place a few brownie pieces at the bottom. Top with a scoop of vanilla ice cream.
3. **Add Hot Fudge**: Drizzle warm hot fudge sauce over the ice cream.
4. **Top**: Add a dollop of whipped cream on top, and garnish with a maraschino cherry and chocolate shavings or sprinkles if desired.

Tips:

- **Brownie Texture**: For fudgier brownies, slightly underbake them; they will continue to set as they cool.
- **Hot Fudge Sauce**: Store leftover hot fudge sauce in an airtight container in the refrigerator. Reheat gently in the microwave or on the stovetop before using.
- **Customization**: Feel free to customize your sundaes with additional toppings like nuts, caramel sauce, or fruit.

Enjoy your Chocolate Fudge Brownie Sundae! It's a delightful, indulgent treat that combines the best of chocolate brownies and classic sundae toppings.

Strawberry Sorbet

Ingredients

- **4 cups (600g) fresh strawberries**, hulled and halved
- **3/4 cup (150g) granulated sugar**
- **1/2 cup (120ml) water**
- **1 tablespoon lemon juice**
- **1/2 teaspoon lemon zest** (optional)

Instructions

1. Prepare the Strawberries:

1. **Hull and Slice**: Remove the stems and hull the strawberries. Slice them in half to help them blend more easily.

2. Make the Strawberry Puree:

1. **Blend Strawberries**: Place the halved strawberries in a blender or food processor. Blend until smooth.
2. **Strain (Optional)**: For a smoother sorbet, strain the strawberry puree through a fine-mesh sieve to remove seeds and any larger bits.

3. Make the Simple Syrup:

1. **Combine Sugar and Water**: In a small saucepan, combine the granulated sugar and water. Heat over medium heat, stirring constantly, until the sugar has completely dissolved. Remove from heat and let it cool to room temperature.

4. Combine Ingredients:

1. **Mix Puree and Syrup**: In a large bowl, combine the strawberry puree, cooled simple syrup, lemon juice, and lemon zest (if using). Stir until well mixed.

5. Chill:

1. **Refrigerate**: Chill the mixture in the refrigerator for at least 1 hour to ensure it's very cold before churning.

6. Churn the Sorbet:

1. **Churn**: Pour the chilled mixture into an ice cream maker and churn according to the manufacturer's instructions, usually for about 20-25 minutes, or until the sorbet reaches a soft-serve consistency.

7. Freeze:

1. **Transfer and Freeze**: Transfer the churned sorbet to an airtight container. Freeze for at least 2 hours or until firm.

8. Serve:

1. **Scoop and Enjoy**: Scoop the sorbet into bowls or cones and enjoy!

Tips:

- **Ripeness of Strawberries**: Use ripe, sweet strawberries for the best flavor. If strawberries are not in season, you can use frozen strawberries.
- **Adjust Sweetness**: Taste the mixture before churning and adjust the sweetness if needed. You can add more sugar or lemon juice to balance the flavor.
- **No Ice Cream Maker?**: If you don't have an ice cream maker, pour the mixture into a shallow dish and freeze. Every 30 minutes, stir the mixture with a fork to break up ice crystals until it reaches the desired consistency.

Enjoy your homemade Strawberry Sorbet! It's a delicious, vibrant treat that captures the essence of fresh strawberries in every bite.

Mango Coconut Ice Cream

Ingredients

- **2 cups (480ml) coconut milk** (full-fat for creaminess)
- **1 cup (240ml) heavy cream**
- **1 cup (240ml) mango puree** (about 2 ripe mangoes, peeled and blended)
- **3/4 cup (150g) granulated sugar**
- **1/4 cup (60ml) light corn syrup** (or honey for a more natural option)
- **1 teaspoon vanilla extract**
- **1/2 teaspoon lime juice** (optional, for a touch of tang)

Instructions

1. Prepare the Mango Puree:

1. **Blend Mangoes**: Peel and dice the mangoes. Blend them in a blender or food processor until smooth. Measure out 1 cup of mango puree.

2. Mix the Base:

1. **Combine Coconut Milk and Cream**: In a large bowl, whisk together the coconut milk and heavy cream until well combined.
2. **Add Sugar and Corn Syrup**: Stir in the granulated sugar and light corn syrup until completely dissolved. This helps to ensure the ice cream is smooth and creamy.
3. **Add Mango Puree and Flavorings**: Mix in the mango puree, vanilla extract, and lime juice (if using). Stir until everything is evenly combined.

3. Chill the Mixture:

1. **Refrigerate**: Cover the mixture and refrigerate for at least 1 hour, or until it's very cold. Chilling the mixture helps it churn better and improves the texture.

4. Churn the Ice Cream:

1. **Churn**: Pour the chilled mixture into an ice cream maker and churn according to the manufacturer's instructions, usually about 20-25 minutes, or until it reaches a soft-serve consistency.

5. Freeze:

1. **Transfer and Freeze**: Transfer the churned ice cream to an airtight container. Freeze for at least 2 hours to firm up the texture.

6. Serve:

1. **Scoop and Enjoy**: Scoop the ice cream into bowls or cones and enjoy your tropical treat!

Tips:

- **Ripeness of Mangoes**: Use ripe, sweet mangoes for the best flavor. If fresh mangoes are not available, you can use frozen mango chunks that have been thawed.
- **Coconut Milk**: For a richer flavor, use full-fat coconut milk. Light coconut milk may result in a less creamy texture.
- **Adjust Sweetness**: Taste the mixture before churning and adjust the sweetness if needed. You can add a little more sugar or honey if desired.

Enjoy your Mango Coconut Ice Cream! It's a delicious and refreshing way to enjoy tropical flavors.

Mint Chocolate Chip Gelato

Ingredients

For the Gelato Base:

- **2 cups (480ml) whole milk**
- **1 cup (240ml) heavy cream**
- **3/4 cup (150g) granulated sugar**
- **4 large egg yolks**
- **1 teaspoon pure vanilla extract**
- **1/2 teaspoon mint extract** (or to taste)
- **A few drops of green food coloring** (optional, for color)

For the Chocolate Chips:

- **1/2 cup (85g) mini chocolate chips** (or finely chopped semisweet chocolate)

Instructions

1. Prepare the Gelato Base:

1. **Heat Milk and Cream**: In a medium saucepan, combine the whole milk and heavy cream. Heat over medium heat until the mixture is hot but not boiling.
2. **Whisk Egg Yolks and Sugar**: In a separate bowl, whisk together the egg yolks and granulated sugar until the mixture is pale and slightly thickened.
3. **Temper the Egg Yolks**: Gradually add a small amount of the hot milk mixture to the egg yolks, whisking constantly to temper them. This helps to prevent the eggs from curdling.
4. **Combine and Cook**: Slowly pour the tempered egg yolk mixture back into the saucepan with the remaining milk mixture. Cook over medium heat, stirring constantly, until the mixture thickens and coats the back of a spoon (170°F-175°F or 77°C-80°C). Do not let it boil.
5. **Cool and Flavor**: Remove from heat and strain the mixture through a fine-mesh sieve into a clean bowl to remove any curdled bits. Stir in the vanilla extract, mint extract, and green food coloring (if using). Let the mixture cool to room temperature.

2. Chill:

1. **Refrigerate**: Cover the bowl with plastic wrap and refrigerate the mixture for at least 4 hours or overnight, until it is very cold.

3. Churn the Gelato:

1. **Churn**: Pour the chilled mixture into an ice cream maker and churn according to the manufacturer's instructions, usually about 20-25 minutes, or until it reaches a soft-serve consistency.

2. **Add Chocolate Chips**: During the last 5 minutes of churning, add the mini chocolate chips or finely chopped chocolate to the gelato, allowing them to distribute evenly.

4. Freeze:

1. **Transfer and Firm**: Transfer the churned gelato to an airtight container and freeze for at least 2 hours to firm up the texture.

5. Serve:

1. **Scoop and Enjoy**: Scoop the gelato into bowls or cones and enjoy!

Tips:

- **Mint Extract**: Be cautious with the amount of mint extract, as it can be quite strong. Start with 1/2 teaspoon and adjust to taste.
- **Food Coloring**: Green food coloring is optional. It's often used to give the gelato that classic minty green hue, but it doesn't affect the flavor.
- **Texture**: For a smoother texture, ensure the gelato mixture is well-chilled before churning and that your ice cream maker's bowl is fully frozen if applicable.

Enjoy your Mint Chocolate Chip Gelato! It's a refreshing and creamy treat with a perfect balance of mint and chocolate.

Raspberry Lemon Sorbet

Ingredients

- **4 cups (600g) fresh raspberries** (or frozen, thawed)
- **1 cup (200g) granulated sugar**
- **1 cup (240ml) water**
- **1/2 cup (120ml) fresh lemon juice** (about 2-3 lemons)
- **1 tablespoon lemon zest** (optional, for extra flavor)
- **1/2 teaspoon vanilla extract** (optional)

Instructions

1. Prepare the Raspberry Puree:

1. **Blend Raspberries**: In a blender or food processor, blend the raspberries until smooth. If using frozen raspberries, make sure they are fully thawed before blending.
2. **Strain (Optional)**: For a smoother texture, strain the raspberry puree through a fine-mesh sieve to remove the seeds.

2. Make the Simple Syrup:

1. **Combine Sugar and Water**: In a small saucepan, combine the granulated sugar and water. Heat over medium heat, stirring constantly, until the sugar has completely dissolved. Remove from heat and let it cool to room temperature.

3. Mix the Sorbet Base:

1. **Combine Ingredients**: In a large bowl, mix the raspberry puree, cooled simple syrup, fresh lemon juice, lemon zest (if using), and vanilla extract (if using). Stir until well combined.

4. Chill:

1. **Refrigerate**: Cover the mixture and refrigerate for at least 1 hour to ensure it is very cold before churning.

5. Churn the Sorbet:

1. **Churn**: Pour the chilled mixture into an ice cream maker and churn according to the manufacturer's instructions, usually about 20-25 minutes, or until it reaches a soft-serve consistency.

6. Freeze:

1. **Transfer and Freeze**: Transfer the churned sorbet to an airtight container and freeze for at least 2 hours to firm up.

7. Serve:

1. **Scoop and Enjoy**: Scoop the sorbet into bowls or cones and enjoy!

Tips:

- **Sweetness Level**: Adjust the sweetness of the sorbet to your taste. You can add more sugar to the simple syrup if needed.
- **Food Processor**: If you don't have a blender, you can use a food processor for making the raspberry puree.
- **Lemon Juice**: Fresh lemon juice is recommended for the best flavor, but bottled lemon juice can be used in a pinch.

Enjoy your homemade Raspberry Lemon Sorbet! It's a vibrant and refreshing dessert that's sure to delight with its perfect balance of tart and sweet.

Classic Vanilla Milkshake

Ingredients

- **2 cups (480ml) vanilla ice cream**
- **1 cup (240ml) whole milk**
- **1 teaspoon vanilla extract**
- **Whipped cream** (optional, for topping)
- **Maraschino cherry** (optional, for garnish)
- **Sprinkles or chocolate shavings** (optional, for garnish)

Instructions

1. Blend the Milkshake:

1. **Combine Ingredients**: In a blender, combine the vanilla ice cream, whole milk, and vanilla extract.
2. **Blend**: Blend on high speed until the mixture is smooth and creamy. You can adjust the thickness by adding more milk if you prefer a thinner consistency or more ice cream for a thicker milkshake.

2. Serve:

1. **Pour**: Pour the milkshake into a tall glass.
2. **Garnish (Optional)**: Top with whipped cream, a maraschino cherry, and sprinkles or chocolate shavings if desired.

Tips:

- **Ice Cream**: Use high-quality vanilla ice cream for the best flavor. You can also use homemade vanilla ice cream for an extra treat.
- **Milk Consistency**: Adjust the amount of milk based on your preference for thickness. For a thicker shake, use less milk; for a thinner shake, use more.
- **Blender**: Make sure your blender is powerful enough to blend the ice cream smoothly. If it struggles, let the ice cream soften slightly before blending.

Enjoy your Classic Vanilla Milkshake! It's a simple and indulgent treat that's always a hit.

Caramel Swirl Ice Cream

Ingredients

For the Vanilla Ice Cream Base:

- 2 cups (480ml) whole milk
- 1 cup (240ml) heavy cream
- 3/4 cup (150g) granulated sugar
- 4 large egg yolks
- 1 teaspoon vanilla extract

For the Caramel Sauce:

- 1 cup (200g) granulated sugar
- 6 tablespoons (85g) unsalted butter
- 1/2 cup (120ml) heavy cream
- 1/4 teaspoon salt (optional, for salted caramel)
- 1 teaspoon vanilla extract

Instructions

1. Prepare the Vanilla Ice Cream Base:

1. **Heat Milk and Cream**: In a medium saucepan, combine the whole milk and heavy cream. Heat over medium heat until the mixture is hot but not boiling.
2. **Whisk Egg Yolks and Sugar**: In a separate bowl, whisk together the egg yolks and granulated sugar until the mixture is pale and slightly thickened.
3. **Temper the Egg Yolks**: Gradually add a small amount of the hot milk mixture to the egg yolks, whisking constantly to temper them. This prevents the eggs from curdling.
4. **Combine and Cook**: Slowly pour the tempered egg yolk mixture back into the saucepan with the remaining milk mixture. Cook over medium heat, stirring constantly, until the mixture thickens and coats the back of a spoon (170°F-175°F or 77°C-80°C). Do not let it boil.
5. **Cool and Flavor**: Remove from heat and strain the mixture through a fine-mesh sieve into a clean bowl. Stir in the vanilla extract. Let the mixture cool to room temperature, then cover and refrigerate until very cold (at least 4 hours or overnight).

2. Make the Caramel Sauce:

1. **Cook Sugar**: In a medium saucepan over medium heat, melt the granulated sugar, stirring constantly until it turns a deep amber color. Be careful not to burn it.
2. **Add Butter**: Once the sugar is melted, carefully add the unsalted butter. The mixture will bubble vigorously.

3. **Add Cream**: Gradually add the heavy cream, continuing to stir until smooth. If making salted caramel, stir in the salt at this stage.
4. **Cool**: Remove from heat and stir in the vanilla extract. Let the caramel sauce cool to room temperature before using.

3. Churn the Ice Cream:

1. **Churn**: Pour the chilled vanilla ice cream base into an ice cream maker and churn according to the manufacturer's instructions, usually about 20-25 minutes, or until it reaches a soft-serve consistency.

4. Swirl in the Caramel:

1. **Layer and Swirl**: Transfer a portion of the churned ice cream to an airtight container. Drizzle some caramel sauce over the ice cream. Add another layer of ice cream and more caramel sauce. Repeat until all the ice cream and caramel are used, swirling gently with a knife or spatula to create the caramel swirls.

5. Freeze:

1. **Firm Up**: Cover the container and freeze the ice cream for at least 2 hours to firm up.

6. Serve:

1. **Scoop and Enjoy**: Scoop the Caramel Swirl Ice Cream into bowls or cones and enjoy!

Tips:

- **Caramel Sauce**: Make the caramel sauce ahead of time and store it in the refrigerator. Reheat gently before swirling it into the ice cream.
- **Ice Cream Maker**: Ensure the ice cream maker's bowl is fully frozen before churning for the best texture.
- **Swirling**: Don't overmix the caramel into the ice cream; you want distinct ribbons of caramel throughout.

Enjoy your homemade Caramel Swirl Ice Cream! It's a creamy and sweet dessert with delightful caramel ribbons in every bite.

Blueberry Cheesecake Ice Cream

Ingredients

For the Blueberry Swirl:

- 2 cups (300g) fresh or frozen blueberries
- 1/2 cup (100g) granulated sugar
- 1 tablespoon lemon juice
- 1/2 teaspoon lemon zest (optional, for extra flavor)

For the Cheesecake Ice Cream Base:

- 2 cups (480ml) whole milk
- 1 cup (240ml) heavy cream
- 3/4 cup (150g) granulated sugar
- 4 large egg yolks
- 1 teaspoon vanilla extract
- 8 ounces (225g) cream cheese, softened and cut into small pieces

Instructions

1. Prepare the Blueberry Swirl:

1. **Cook Blueberries**: In a medium saucepan, combine the blueberries, granulated sugar, and lemon juice. Cook over medium heat, stirring frequently, until the blueberries break down and the mixture thickens into a syrup (about 10-15 minutes).
2. **Add Lemon Zest**: If using, stir in the lemon zest. Remove from heat and let the blueberry mixture cool to room temperature. You can blend it slightly if you prefer a smoother texture or leave it chunky.

2. Prepare the Cheesecake Ice Cream Base:

1. **Heat Milk and Cream**: In a medium saucepan, combine the whole milk and heavy cream. Heat over medium heat until the mixture is hot but not boiling.
2. **Whisk Egg Yolks and Sugar**: In a separate bowl, whisk together the egg yolks and granulated sugar until the mixture is pale and slightly thickened.
3. **Temper the Egg Yolks**: Gradually add a small amount of the hot milk mixture to the egg yolks, whisking constantly to temper them. This prevents the eggs from curdling.
4. **Combine and Cook**: Slowly pour the tempered egg yolk mixture back into the saucepan with the remaining milk mixture. Cook over medium heat, stirring constantly, until the mixture thickens and coats the back of a spoon (170°F-175°F or 77°C-80°C). Do not let it boil.
5. **Add Cream Cheese**: Remove from heat and strain the mixture through a fine-mesh sieve into a clean bowl. Add the softened cream cheese and stir until completely smooth.

Stir in the vanilla extract. Let the mixture cool to room temperature, then cover and refrigerate until very cold (at least 4 hours or overnight).

3. Churn the Ice Cream:

1. **Churn**: Pour the chilled cheesecake ice cream base into an ice cream maker and churn according to the manufacturer's instructions, usually about 20-25 minutes, or until it reaches a soft-serve consistency.

4. Swirl in the Blueberry Sauce:

1. **Layer and Swirl**: Transfer a portion of the churned ice cream to an airtight container. Drizzle some of the cooled blueberry sauce over the ice cream. Add another layer of ice cream and more blueberry sauce. Repeat until all the ice cream and blueberry sauce are used, swirling gently with a knife or spatula to create a marbled effect.

5. Freeze:

1. **Firm Up**: Cover the container and freeze the ice cream for at least 2 hours to firm up.

6. Serve:

1. **Scoop and Enjoy**: Scoop the Blueberry Cheesecake Ice Cream into bowls or cones and enjoy!

Tips:

- **Cheesecake Base**: Make sure the cream cheese is well-softened and fully incorporated into the ice cream base for a smooth texture.
- **Blueberry Sauce**: You can make the blueberry sauce ahead of time and store it in the refrigerator. Reheat gently if needed before swirling it into the ice cream.
- **Ice Cream Maker**: Ensure the ice cream maker's bowl is fully frozen before churning for the best texture.

Enjoy your homemade Blueberry Cheesecake Ice Cream! It's a creamy and fruity dessert with a delightful blend of cheesecake and blueberry flavors.

Mocha Almond Fudge

Ingredients

For the Mocha Ice Cream Base:

- **2 cups (480ml) whole milk**
- **1 cup (240ml) heavy cream**
- **3/4 cup (150g) granulated sugar**
- **1/2 cup (120ml) strong brewed coffee** (cooled)
- **4 large egg yolks**
- **1 teaspoon vanilla extract**
- **1/4 cup (30g) cocoa powder** (unsweetened)
- **1/2 cup (85g) semisweet chocolate chips** (optional, for extra chocolatey goodness)

For the Fudge Swirl:

- **1 cup (200g) semisweet chocolate chips**
- **1/2 cup (120ml) heavy cream**
- **1 tablespoon unsalted butter**

For the Almonds:

- **1 cup (140g) toasted almonds** (slivered or chopped)

Instructions

1. Prepare the Mocha Ice Cream Base:

1. **Heat Milk and Cream**: In a medium saucepan, combine the whole milk and heavy cream. Heat over medium heat until the mixture is hot but not boiling.
2. **Whisk Cocoa Powder and Sugar**: In a separate bowl, whisk together the cocoa powder and granulated sugar.
3. **Combine Cocoa and Milk**: Gradually add the cocoa powder mixture to the hot milk mixture, stirring until well combined.
4. **Whisk Egg Yolks and Add Coffee**: In another bowl, whisk together the egg yolks. Gradually add a small amount of the hot cocoa mixture to the egg yolks, whisking constantly to temper them.
5. **Cook Custard**: Slowly pour the tempered egg yolks back into the saucepan with the remaining cocoa mixture. Cook over medium heat, stirring constantly, until the mixture thickens and coats the back of a spoon (170°F-175°F or 77°C-80°C). Do not let it boil.
6. **Add Coffee and Chocolate Chips**: Remove from heat and strain the mixture through a fine-mesh sieve into a clean bowl. Stir in the brewed coffee, vanilla extract, and chocolate chips (if using). Let the mixture cool to room temperature, then cover and refrigerate until very cold (at least 4 hours or overnight).

2. Make the Fudge Swirl:

1. **Heat Cream and Butter**: In a small saucepan, heat the heavy cream and unsalted butter over medium heat until the butter is melted.
2. **Add Chocolate Chips**: Remove from heat and stir in the semisweet chocolate chips until smooth and glossy. Let it cool slightly before using.

3. Churn the Ice Cream:

1. **Churn**: Pour the chilled mocha ice cream base into an ice cream maker and churn according to the manufacturer's instructions, usually about 20-25 minutes, or until it reaches a soft-serve consistency.

4. Add Fudge and Almonds:

1. **Layer and Swirl**: Transfer a portion of the churned ice cream to an airtight container. Drizzle some of the fudge sauce over the ice cream. Add a layer of toasted almonds. Add another layer of ice cream, more fudge sauce, and almonds. Repeat until all the ice cream, fudge, and almonds are used, gently swirling with a knife or spatula to distribute the fudge and almonds throughout the ice cream.

5. Freeze:

1. **Firm Up**: Cover the container and freeze the ice cream for at least 2 hours to firm up.

6. Serve:

1. **Scoop and Enjoy**: Scoop the Mocha Almond Fudge Ice Cream into bowls or cones and enjoy!

Tips:

- **Coffee Strength**: Use strong brewed coffee for a pronounced coffee flavor. Adjust the amount based on your preference.
- **Chocolate Chips**: Adding chocolate chips to the ice cream base enhances the chocolate flavor and adds texture.
- **Fudge Consistency**: If the fudge swirl is too thick after cooling, gently reheat it to make it easier to swirl into the ice cream.

Enjoy your homemade Mocha Almond Fudge Ice Cream! It's a delightful combination of rich mocha flavor, creamy fudge, and crunchy almonds.

Peach Frozen Yogurt

Ingredients

- **2 cups (300g) fresh peaches** (peeled, pitted, and diced, or about 2-3 medium peaches)
- **1/2 cup (100g) granulated sugar** (adjust to taste)
- **1 cup (240ml) plain Greek yogurt** (or regular yogurt)
- **1/2 cup (120ml) heavy cream**
- **1 tablespoon lemon juice** (optional, for added brightness)
- **1 teaspoon vanilla extract** (optional)

Instructions

1. Prepare the Peach Puree:

1. **Blend Peaches**: Place the diced peaches in a blender or food processor. Blend until smooth. If you prefer a smoother texture, you can strain the puree through a fine-mesh sieve to remove any larger pieces.
2. **Sweeten**: In a bowl, mix the peach puree with the granulated sugar. Stir until the sugar is fully dissolved. Adjust the sweetness to your taste.

2. Mix the Frozen Yogurt Base:

1. **Combine Ingredients**: In a large bowl, combine the peach puree, Greek yogurt, and heavy cream. Mix until well combined.
2. **Add Flavorings**: Stir in the lemon juice and vanilla extract if using. These ingredients enhance the flavor and add depth.

3. Chill the Mixture:

1. **Refrigerate**: Cover the mixture and refrigerate for at least 1 hour. This helps the mixture chill thoroughly, which improves the texture when churning.

4. Churn the Frozen Yogurt:

1. **Churn**: Pour the chilled mixture into an ice cream maker. Churn according to the manufacturer's instructions, usually for about 20-25 minutes, until it reaches a soft-serve consistency.

5. Freeze:

1. **Firm Up**: Transfer the churned frozen yogurt to an airtight container. Freeze for at least 2 hours to firm up further.

6. Serve:

1. **Scoop and Enjoy**: Scoop the Peach Frozen Yogurt into bowls or cones and enjoy!

Tips:

- **Peach Selection**: Use ripe, juicy peaches for the best flavor. If fresh peaches are not available, thawed frozen peaches work well too.
- **Smoothness**: For a smoother texture, you can strain the peach puree to remove any bits of fruit.
- **Sweetness Level**: Adjust the amount of sugar based on the sweetness of the peaches and your personal preference.

Enjoy your refreshing Peach Frozen Yogurt! It's a great way to enjoy the flavors of summer year-round.

Matcha Green Tea Ice Cream

Ingredients

- 2 cups (480ml) whole milk
- 1 cup (240ml) heavy cream
- 3/4 cup (150g) granulated sugar
- 4 large egg yolks
- 2 tablespoons matcha green tea powder
- 1 teaspoon vanilla extract

Instructions

1. Prepare the Matcha Base:

1. **Heat Milk and Cream**: In a medium saucepan, combine the whole milk and heavy cream. Heat over medium heat until the mixture is hot but not boiling.
2. **Whisk Matcha and Sugar**: In a separate bowl, whisk together the matcha green tea powder and granulated sugar. You may need to sift the matcha to remove any lumps.
3. **Combine Matcha with Milk**: Gradually whisk the matcha mixture into the hot milk and cream mixture until fully dissolved.
4. **Whisk Egg Yolks**: In another bowl, whisk the egg yolks until they are light and slightly thickened.
5. **Temper the Egg Yolks**: Gradually add a small amount of the hot milk mixture to the egg yolks, whisking constantly to temper them.
6. **Cook Custard**: Slowly pour the tempered egg yolks back into the saucepan with the remaining milk mixture. Cook over medium heat, stirring constantly, until the mixture thickens and coats the back of a spoon (170°F-175°F or 77°C-80°C). Do not let it boil.
7. **Strain and Cool**: Remove from heat and strain the mixture through a fine-mesh sieve into a clean bowl to remove any bits of cooked egg. Stir in the vanilla extract. Let the mixture cool to room temperature, then cover and refrigerate until very cold (at least 4 hours or overnight).

2. Churn the Ice Cream:

1. **Churn**: Pour the chilled mixture into an ice cream maker and churn according to the manufacturer's instructions, usually about 20-25 minutes, or until it reaches a soft-serve consistency.

3. Freeze:

1. **Firm Up**: Transfer the churned ice cream to an airtight container and freeze for at least 2 hours to firm up.

4. Serve:

1. **Scoop and Enjoy**: Scoop the Matcha Green Tea Ice Cream into bowls or cones and enjoy!

Tips:

- **Matcha Quality**: Use high-quality matcha green tea powder for the best flavor and vibrant color. Culinary-grade matcha works well for ice cream.
- **Smoothness**: Ensure the matcha is thoroughly mixed with the milk to avoid any lumps in the ice cream.
- **Ice Cream Maker**: Make sure the ice cream maker's bowl is fully frozen before churning for the best texture.

Enjoy your homemade Matcha Green Tea Ice Cream! It's a refreshing and unique treat that combines the rich flavor of green tea with the creamy indulgence of ice cream.

Pineapple Coconut Sorbet

Ingredients

- **2 cups (280g) fresh pineapple** (peeled, cored, and diced, or about 1 medium pineapple)
- **1 cup (240ml) coconut milk** (full-fat for creaminess)
- **1/2 cup (100g) granulated sugar** (adjust to taste)
- **1 tablespoon lime juice** (optional, for added brightness)
- **1/2 teaspoon vanilla extract** (optional)

Instructions

1. Prepare the Pineapple Puree:

1. **Blend Pineapple**: Place the diced pineapple in a blender or food processor. Blend until smooth. If you prefer a smoother texture, you can strain the puree through a fine-mesh sieve to remove any pulp.
2. **Sweeten**: In a bowl, mix the pineapple puree with the granulated sugar. Stir until the sugar is fully dissolved. Adjust the sweetness according to your taste.

2. Combine Ingredients:

1. **Mix**: In a large bowl, combine the pineapple puree with the coconut milk. Stir well until fully incorporated.
2. **Add Lime and Vanilla**: Stir in the lime juice and vanilla extract if using. These ingredients add a bright note and enhance the overall flavor.

3. Chill the Mixture:

1. **Refrigerate**: Cover the mixture and refrigerate for at least 1 hour to ensure it is very cold before churning. This helps with the freezing process and improves texture.

4. Churn the Sorbet:

1. **Churn**: Pour the chilled mixture into an ice cream maker and churn according to the manufacturer's instructions, usually about 20-25 minutes, or until it reaches a soft-serve consistency.

5. Freeze:

1. **Firm Up**: Transfer the churned sorbet to an airtight container and freeze for at least 2 hours to firm up.

6. Serve:

1. **Scoop and Enjoy**: Scoop the Pineapple Coconut Sorbet into bowls or cones and enjoy!

Tips:

- **Pineapple**: Use ripe, sweet pineapple for the best flavor. If using canned pineapple, choose unsweetened pineapple and adjust the sugar accordingly.
- **Texture**: For a smoother sorbet, ensure the pineapple is blended well and strained if necessary.
- **Coconut Milk**: Full-fat coconut milk provides a creamy texture, but you can use light coconut milk if you prefer a lighter option.

Enjoy your homemade Pineapple Coconut Sorbet! It's a refreshing, tropical dessert that's perfect for cooling off on a hot day.

Espresso Affogato

Ingredients

- **2 scoops vanilla ice cream** (or gelato for a creamier texture)
- **1 shot (1 ounce or 30ml) hot espresso** (or strong brewed coffee)
- **Optional**: A drizzle of chocolate syrup or caramel sauce
- **Optional**: A sprinkle of cocoa powder or shaved chocolate for garnish

Instructions

1. Prepare the Espresso:

1. **Brew Espresso**: Brew a fresh shot of espresso using an espresso machine or a strong coffee using a coffee maker. The espresso should be hot when poured over the ice cream.

2. Serve the Ice Cream:

1. **Scoop Ice Cream**: Place two scoops of vanilla ice cream in a serving glass or bowl. You can use a single scoop if you prefer a smaller portion.

3. Pour Espresso:

1. **Affogato**: Immediately pour the hot espresso over the ice cream. The hot espresso will start to melt the ice cream, creating a delicious blend of creamy and coffee flavors.

4. Optional Garnishes:

1. **Drizzle and Garnish**: If desired, drizzle with chocolate syrup or caramel sauce. You can also sprinkle with cocoa powder or shaved chocolate for extra flavor and texture.

5. Serve:

1. **Enjoy**: Serve the Espresso Affogato immediately while the ice cream is still cold and the espresso is hot.

Tips:

- **Ice Cream**: Use high-quality vanilla ice cream or gelato for the best results. The vanilla flavor complements the espresso perfectly.
- **Espresso**: If you don't have an espresso machine, you can use a strong brewed coffee as a substitute. The key is to make sure it's hot and strong.
- **Customize**: Feel free to experiment with different flavors of ice cream or add a splash of liqueur for a grown-up twist.

Enjoy your Espresso Affogato! It's a perfect blend of coffee and creaminess, making it an elegant and satisfying dessert.

Cookie Dough Ice Cream

Ingredients

For the Ice Cream Base:

- 2 cups (480ml) whole milk
- 1 cup (240ml) heavy cream
- 3/4 cup (150g) granulated sugar
- 4 large egg yolks
- 1 teaspoon vanilla extract

For the Cookie Dough:

- 1/2 cup (1 stick or 115g) unsalted butter, softened
- 1/2 cup (100g) granulated sugar
- 1/2 cup (110g) packed brown sugar
- 1/2 teaspoon vanilla extract
- 1 cup (130g) all-purpose flour
- 1/4 teaspoon salt
- 1/4 cup (60ml) milk
- 1/2 cup (90g) mini chocolate chips

Instructions

1. Prepare the Cookie Dough:

1. **Cream Butter and Sugars**: In a medium bowl, beat the softened butter, granulated sugar, and brown sugar until light and fluffy.
2. **Add Vanilla**: Stir in the vanilla extract.
3. **Combine Dry Ingredients**: In another bowl, whisk together the flour and salt.
4. **Mix**: Gradually add the dry ingredients to the butter mixture, alternating with the milk, until well combined. Fold in the mini chocolate chips.
5. **Chill Dough**: Scoop the cookie dough onto a parchment-lined baking sheet, breaking it into small chunks. Freeze for about 30 minutes to firm up.

2. Make the Ice Cream Base:

1. **Heat Milk and Cream**: In a medium saucepan, combine the whole milk and heavy cream. Heat over medium heat until the mixture is hot but not boiling.
2. **Whisk Egg Yolks and Sugar**: In a separate bowl, whisk the egg yolks and granulated sugar until the mixture is pale and slightly thickened.
3. **Temper the Egg Yolks**: Gradually add a small amount of the hot milk mixture to the egg yolks, whisking constantly to temper them.

4. **Cook Custard**: Slowly pour the tempered egg yolks back into the saucepan with the remaining milk mixture. Cook over medium heat, stirring constantly, until the mixture thickens and coats the back of a spoon (170°F-175°F or 77°C-80°C). Do not let it boil.
5. **Strain and Cool**: Remove from heat and strain the mixture through a fine-mesh sieve into a clean bowl. Stir in the vanilla extract. Let it cool to room temperature, then cover and refrigerate until very cold (at least 4 hours or overnight).

3. Churn the Ice Cream:

1. **Churn**: Pour the chilled ice cream base into an ice cream maker and churn according to the manufacturer's instructions, usually about 20-25 minutes, or until it reaches a soft-serve consistency.
2. **Add Cookie Dough**: Gently fold in the chilled cookie dough chunks during the last 5 minutes of churning.

4. Freeze:

1. **Firm Up**: Transfer the churned ice cream to an airtight container. Freeze for at least 2 hours to firm up.

5. Serve:

1. **Scoop and Enjoy**: Scoop the Cookie Dough Ice Cream into bowls or cones and enjoy!

Tips:

- **Cookie Dough**: Make sure the cookie dough is firm but not too hard before adding it to the ice cream. Small chunks work best.
- **Ice Cream Maker**: Ensure the ice cream maker's bowl is fully frozen before churning for the best texture.
- **Substitutes**: You can use store-bought cookie dough if you prefer, but homemade dough has the best flavor and texture.

Enjoy your homemade Cookie Dough Ice Cream! It's a creamy, indulgent treat with chunks of delicious cookie dough that make it truly irresistible.

Peanut Butter Cup Ice Cream

Ingredients

For the Ice Cream Base:

- **2 cups (480ml) whole milk**
- **1 cup (240ml) heavy cream**
- **3/4 cup (150g) granulated sugar**
- **4 large egg yolks**
- **1/2 cup (120g) creamy peanut butter**
- **1 teaspoon vanilla extract**

For the Peanut Butter Cup Swirl:

- **1 cup (180g) mini peanut butter cups** (chopped into small pieces)
- **1/2 cup (120ml) hot fudge sauce** (store-bought or homemade, optional for extra chocolate swirl)

Instructions

1. Prepare the Ice Cream Base:

1. **Heat Milk and Cream**: In a medium saucepan, combine the whole milk and heavy cream. Heat over medium heat until the mixture is hot but not boiling.
2. **Whisk Egg Yolks and Sugar**: In a separate bowl, whisk the egg yolks and granulated sugar until the mixture is light and slightly thickened.
3. **Temper the Egg Yolks**: Gradually add a small amount of the hot milk mixture to the egg yolks, whisking constantly to temper them.
4. **Cook Custard**: Slowly pour the tempered egg yolks back into the saucepan with the remaining milk mixture. Cook over medium heat, stirring constantly, until the mixture thickens and coats the back of a spoon (170°F-175°F or 77°C-80°C). Do not let it boil.
5. **Add Peanut Butter**: Remove from heat and strain the mixture through a fine-mesh sieve into a clean bowl. Stir in the peanut butter until fully combined. Add the vanilla extract and stir again. Let the mixture cool to room temperature, then cover and refrigerate until very cold (at least 4 hours or overnight).

2. Churn the Ice Cream:

1. **Churn**: Pour the chilled mixture into an ice cream maker and churn according to the manufacturer's instructions, usually about 20-25 minutes, or until it reaches a soft-serve consistency.
2. **Add Peanut Butter Cups**: During the last 5 minutes of churning, gently fold in the chopped mini peanut butter cups. If using hot fudge sauce, you can swirl it in at this stage as well.

3. Freeze:

1. **Firm Up**: Transfer the churned ice cream to an airtight container. If you're using hot fudge sauce, you can swirl some into the ice cream as you transfer it. Freeze for at least 2 hours to firm up.

4. Serve:

1. **Scoop and Enjoy**: Scoop the Peanut Butter Cup Ice Cream into bowls or cones and enjoy!

Tips:

- **Peanut Butter**: Use creamy peanut butter for a smooth texture. Natural peanut butter can be used, but it may cause slight texture differences.
- **Hot Fudge Sauce**: If you prefer a chocolate swirl, ensure the fudge sauce is warm but not hot when adding to the ice cream to prevent it from hardening immediately.
- **Ice Cream Maker**: Ensure the ice cream maker's bowl is fully frozen before churning to achieve the best texture.

Enjoy your homemade Peanut Butter Cup Ice Cream! It's a decadent, creamy treat that combines the best of peanut butter and chocolate for a truly delightful dessert.

Lemon Basil Sorbet

Ingredients

- **1 cup (240ml) water**
- **1 cup (200g) granulated sugar**
- **1 cup (240ml) freshly squeezed lemon juice** (about 4-6 lemons)
- **1/2 cup (120ml) fresh basil leaves**, packed
- **1 tablespoon lemon zest** (optional, for extra lemony flavor)

Instructions

1. Make the Basil Syrup:

1. **Prepare the Basil**: In a saucepan, combine the water and granulated sugar. Heat over medium heat, stirring occasionally, until the sugar is fully dissolved to create a simple syrup.
2. **Infuse with Basil**: Remove the saucepan from heat. Add the fresh basil leaves to the syrup, stirring gently. Let the basil steep in the syrup for about 30 minutes, allowing the basil flavor to infuse into the syrup.
3. **Strain**: Strain the basil syrup through a fine-mesh sieve to remove the basil leaves. Let the syrup cool to room temperature.

2. Prepare the Sorbet Mixture:

1. **Combine Ingredients**: In a large bowl, combine the basil syrup with the freshly squeezed lemon juice. If using, add the lemon zest for an extra burst of lemon flavor.
2. **Mix Well**: Stir the mixture until well combined. Taste and adjust the sweetness or tartness if needed by adding more sugar or lemon juice.

3. Chill the Mixture:

1. **Refrigerate**: Cover the mixture and refrigerate for at least 1 hour to ensure it is very cold before churning. This helps with the freezing process and improves texture.

4. Churn the Sorbet:

1. **Churn**: Pour the chilled mixture into an ice cream maker and churn according to the manufacturer's instructions, usually about 20-25 minutes, or until it reaches a soft-serve consistency.

5. Freeze:

1. **Firm Up**: Transfer the churned sorbet to an airtight container. Freeze for at least 2 hours to firm up.

6. Serve:

1. **Scoop and Enjoy**: Scoop the Lemon Basil Sorbet into bowls or cones and enjoy!

Tips:

- **Basil Freshness**: Use fresh basil for the best flavor. Dried basil will not provide the same vibrant taste.
- **Lemon Juice**: Freshly squeezed lemon juice is preferred for its bright, tangy flavor.
- **Texture**: Ensure the sorbet mixture is well-chilled before churning to get a smoother texture.

Enjoy your homemade Lemon Basil Sorbet! It's a sophisticated and refreshing dessert that beautifully balances tart lemon and aromatic basil.

Chocolate Mint Ice Cream

Ingredients

For the Ice Cream Base:

- **2 cups (480ml) whole milk**
- **1 cup (240ml) heavy cream**
- **3/4 cup (150g) granulated sugar**
- **4 large egg yolks**
- **1 teaspoon vanilla extract**
- **1/2 cup (120ml) unsweetened cocoa powder**

For the Mint Flavor:

- **1/2 cup (120ml) fresh mint leaves**, packed
- **1/2 teaspoon peppermint extract** (adjust to taste)
- **1/2 cup (90g) mini chocolate chips** (optional, for added texture)

Instructions

1. Infuse the Milk:

1. **Heat Milk and Mint**: In a medium saucepan, combine the whole milk and fresh mint leaves. Heat over medium heat until the mixture is hot but not boiling. Remove from heat and let the mint steep in the milk for about 30 minutes to infuse its flavor.
2. **Strain**: After steeping, strain the mint leaves from the milk using a fine-mesh sieve.

2. Prepare the Ice Cream Base:

1. **Mix Cocoa Powder**: Return the mint-infused milk to the saucepan and whisk in the unsweetened cocoa powder until fully dissolved.
2. **Heat Milk and Cream**: Add the heavy cream to the cocoa mixture and heat until the mixture is hot but not boiling.
3. **Whisk Egg Yolks and Sugar**: In a separate bowl, whisk the egg yolks and granulated sugar until the mixture is light and slightly thickened.
4. **Temper the Egg Yolks**: Gradually add a small amount of the hot milk mixture to the egg yolks, whisking constantly to temper them.
5. **Cook Custard**: Slowly pour the tempered egg yolks back into the saucepan with the remaining milk mixture. Cook over medium heat, stirring constantly, until the mixture thickens and coats the back of a spoon (170°F-175°F or 77°C-80°C). Do not let it boil.
6. **Cool the Mixture**: Remove from heat and strain the custard through a fine-mesh sieve into a clean bowl. Stir in the vanilla extract and peppermint extract. Let the mixture cool to room temperature, then cover and refrigerate until very cold (at least 4 hours or overnight).

3. Churn the Ice Cream:

1. **Churn**: Pour the chilled mixture into an ice cream maker and churn according to the manufacturer's instructions, usually about 20-25 minutes, or until it reaches a soft-serve consistency.
2. **Add Chocolate Chips**: During the last 5 minutes of churning, gently fold in the mini chocolate chips if using.

4. Freeze:

1. **Firm Up**: Transfer the churned ice cream to an airtight container and freeze for at least 2 hours to firm up.

5. Serve:

1. **Scoop and Enjoy**: Scoop the Chocolate Mint Ice Cream into bowls or cones and enjoy!

Tips:

- **Mint Flavor**: Adjust the amount of peppermint extract based on your preference for mint intensity. Peppermint extract is quite strong, so start with a smaller amount and add more if desired.
- **Cocoa Powder**: Use high-quality unsweetened cocoa powder for a rich chocolate flavor.
- **Ice Cream Maker**: Ensure the ice cream maker's bowl is fully frozen before churning for the best texture.

Enjoy your homemade Chocolate Mint Ice Cream! It's a cool and refreshing treat that combines the best of chocolate and mint flavors in every bite.

Blackberry Sage Sorbet

Ingredients

- **2 cups (300g) fresh blackberries** (or frozen, thawed)
- **1 cup (200g) granulated sugar**
- **1 cup (240ml) water**
- **1/2 cup (120ml) fresh lemon juice** (about 2-3 lemons)
- **1/4 cup (60ml) fresh sage leaves** (about 10-12 leaves)

Instructions

1. Make the Sage Syrup:

1. **Prepare Syrup**: In a saucepan, combine the water and granulated sugar. Heat over medium heat, stirring occasionally, until the sugar is fully dissolved to create a simple syrup.
2. **Infuse with Sage**: Remove from heat and add the fresh sage leaves to the syrup. Stir gently and let the sage steep in the syrup for about 30 minutes to infuse its flavor.
3. **Strain**: Strain the sage syrup through a fine-mesh sieve to remove the sage leaves. Let it cool to room temperature.

2. Prepare the Blackberry Puree:

1. **Blend Blackberries**: Place the blackberries in a blender or food processor and blend until smooth. If you prefer a smoother texture, you can strain the puree through a fine-mesh sieve to remove the seeds.
2. **Combine with Lemon Juice**: In a large bowl, combine the blackberry puree with the lemon juice.

3. Combine Ingredients:

1. **Mix**: Stir the cooled sage syrup into the blackberry and lemon mixture. Mix until well combined.
2. **Taste and Adjust**: Taste the mixture and adjust the sweetness or tartness if needed by adding more sugar or lemon juice.

4. Chill the Mixture:

1. **Refrigerate**: Cover the mixture and refrigerate for at least 1 hour to ensure it is very cold before churning. This helps with the freezing process and improves texture.

5. Churn the Sorbet:

1. **Churn**: Pour the chilled mixture into an ice cream maker and churn according to the manufacturer's instructions, usually about 20-25 minutes, or until it reaches a soft-serve consistency.

6. Freeze:

1. **Firm Up**: Transfer the churned sorbet to an airtight container and freeze for at least 2 hours to firm up.

7. Serve:

1. **Scoop and Enjoy**: Scoop the Blackberry Sage Sorbet into bowls or cones and enjoy!

Tips:

- **Blackberries**: Use ripe, sweet blackberries for the best flavor. If using frozen blackberries, make sure they are thawed before blending.
- **Sage**: Fresh sage provides a subtle, aromatic flavor. Dried sage is not a good substitute as it lacks the fresh, vibrant notes.
- **Texture**: For a smoother texture, strain the blackberry puree to remove seeds. You can also strain the sorbet after churning if you want an extra smooth result.

Enjoy your Blackberry Sage Sorbet! It's a refreshing and elegant dessert that beautifully combines fruity and herbal flavors.

Salted Caramel Gelato

Ingredients

For the Caramel Base:

- 1 cup (200g) granulated sugar
- 1/4 cup (60ml) water
- 1/2 cup (120ml) heavy cream
- 1/4 cup (60ml) whole milk
- 1/4 cup (55g) unsalted butter
- 1/2 teaspoon sea salt (adjust to taste)

For the Gelato Base:

- 2 cups (480ml) whole milk
- 1 cup (240ml) heavy cream
- 3/4 cup (150g) granulated sugar
- 4 large egg yolks
- 1 teaspoon vanilla extract

Instructions

1. Make the Caramel Sauce:

1. **Cook Sugar**: In a medium saucepan, combine the granulated sugar and water. Heat over medium heat, stirring occasionally until the sugar is dissolved. Continue cooking without stirring until the mixture turns a deep amber color.
2. **Add Cream and Butter**: Remove from heat and carefully add the heavy cream and butter (the mixture will bubble vigorously). Stir until smooth.
3. **Season**: Stir in the sea salt. Let the caramel sauce cool to room temperature.

2. Prepare the Gelato Base:

1. **Heat Milk and Cream**: In a medium saucepan, combine the whole milk and heavy cream. Heat over medium heat until the mixture is hot but not boiling.
2. **Whisk Egg Yolks and Sugar**: In a separate bowl, whisk the egg yolks and granulated sugar until light and slightly thickened.
3. **Temper the Egg Yolks**: Gradually add a small amount of the hot milk mixture to the egg yolks, whisking constantly to temper them.
4. **Cook Custard**: Slowly pour the tempered egg yolks back into the saucepan with the remaining milk mixture. Cook over medium heat, stirring constantly, until the mixture thickens and coats the back of a spoon (170°F-175°F or 77°C-80°C). Do not let it boil.

5. **Strain and Cool**: Remove from heat and strain the custard through a fine-mesh sieve into a clean bowl. Stir in the vanilla extract. Let it cool to room temperature, then cover and refrigerate until very cold (at least 4 hours or overnight).

3. Incorporate Caramel:

1. **Swirl in Caramel**: Once the gelato base is chilled, stir in about 1/2 cup of the cooled caramel sauce. You can reserve some caramel sauce for drizzling or swirling into the gelato after churning.

4. Churn the Gelato:

1. **Churn**: Pour the mixture into an ice cream maker and churn according to the manufacturer's instructions, usually about 20-25 minutes, or until it reaches a soft-serve consistency.
2. **Swirl Extra Caramel**: During the last 5 minutes of churning, gently swirl in any reserved caramel sauce if desired.

5. Freeze:

1. **Firm Up**: Transfer the churned gelato to an airtight container and freeze for at least 2 hours to firm up.

6. Serve:

1. **Scoop and Enjoy**: Scoop the Salted Caramel Gelato into bowls or cones and enjoy!

Tips:

- **Caramel**: Be careful when making caramel as it can burn quickly. If you're new to caramel-making, keep a close eye on it to avoid burning.
- **Sea Salt**: Adjust the amount of sea salt to your taste. A little goes a long way in enhancing the caramel flavor.
- **Ice Cream Maker**: Ensure the ice cream maker's bowl is fully frozen before churning for the best texture.

Enjoy your homemade Salted Caramel Gelato! It's a rich and creamy dessert with the perfect balance of sweet and salty flavors.

Pumpkin Spice Ice Cream

Ingredients

For the Ice Cream Base:

- 1 cup (240ml) whole milk
- 1 cup (240ml) heavy cream
- 3/4 cup (150g) granulated sugar
- 1/2 cup (120g) canned pumpkin puree (not pumpkin pie filling)
- 4 large egg yolks
- 1 teaspoon vanilla extract

For the Pumpkin Spice Mixture:

- 1 teaspoon ground cinnamon
- 1/2 teaspoon ground ginger
- 1/4 teaspoon ground nutmeg
- 1/4 teaspoon ground cloves

Instructions

1. Prepare the Pumpkin Spice Mixture:

1. **Mix Spices**: In a small bowl, combine the ground cinnamon, ground ginger, ground nutmeg, and ground cloves. Set aside.

2. Prepare the Ice Cream Base:

1. **Heat Milk and Cream**: In a medium saucepan, combine the whole milk and heavy cream. Heat over medium heat until the mixture is hot but not boiling.
2. **Whisk Egg Yolks and Sugar**: In a separate bowl, whisk the egg yolks and granulated sugar until the mixture is light and slightly thickened.
3. **Temper the Egg Yolks**: Gradually add a small amount of the hot milk mixture to the egg yolks, whisking constantly to temper them.
4. **Cook Custard**: Slowly pour the tempered egg yolks back into the saucepan with the remaining milk mixture. Cook over medium heat, stirring constantly, until the mixture thickens and coats the back of a spoon (170°F-175°F or 77°C-80°C). Do not let it boil.
5. **Add Pumpkin and Spices**: Remove from heat and strain the custard through a fine-mesh sieve into a clean bowl. Stir in the pumpkin puree and the pumpkin spice mixture until fully combined.
6. **Cool and Chill**: Stir in the vanilla extract. Let the mixture cool to room temperature, then cover and refrigerate until very cold (at least 4 hours or overnight).

3. Churn the Ice Cream:

1. **Churn**: Pour the chilled mixture into an ice cream maker and churn according to the manufacturer's instructions, usually about 20-25 minutes, or until it reaches a soft-serve consistency.

4. Freeze:

1. **Firm Up**: Transfer the churned ice cream to an airtight container and freeze for at least 2 hours to firm up.

5. Serve:

1. **Scoop and Enjoy**: Scoop the Pumpkin Spice Ice Cream into bowls or cones and enjoy!

Tips:

- **Pumpkin Puree**: Use plain canned pumpkin puree for the best flavor. Avoid pumpkin pie filling, which contains added spices and sugar.
- **Spices**: Adjust the spices to your taste. You can add a pinch more of any spice if you prefer a stronger flavor.
- **Texture**: Ensure the ice cream base is well-chilled before churning for the smoothest texture.

Enjoy your homemade Pumpkin Spice Ice Cream! It's a creamy, spiced treat that captures the essence of fall in every bite.

Pina Colada Sorbet

Ingredients

- **2 cups (480ml) pineapple juice** (preferably fresh or 100% juice)
- **1 cup (240ml) coconut milk** (canned, full-fat for creaminess)
- **1 cup (200g) granulated sugar**
- **1/4 cup (60ml) fresh lime juice** (about 2 limes)
- **1/2 teaspoon vanilla extract** (optional)
- **1/4 cup (60ml) rum** (optional, for a true Pina Colada flavor)

Instructions

1. Prepare the Mixture:

1. **Combine Ingredients**: In a large bowl, whisk together the pineapple juice, coconut milk, granulated sugar, and fresh lime juice. If using vanilla extract, add it to the mixture. If you're adding rum, stir it in at this stage as well.
2. **Mix Until Dissolved**: Stir the mixture until the sugar is fully dissolved.

2. Chill the Mixture:

1. **Refrigerate**: Cover the mixture and refrigerate for at least 1 hour to ensure it is very cold before churning. This helps with the freezing process and improves texture.

3. Churn the Sorbet:

1. **Churn**: Pour the chilled mixture into an ice cream maker and churn according to the manufacturer's instructions, usually about 20-25 minutes, or until it reaches a soft-serve consistency.

4. Freeze:

1. **Firm Up**: Transfer the churned sorbet to an airtight container and freeze for at least 2 hours to firm up.

5. Serve:

1. **Scoop and Enjoy**: Scoop the Pina Colada Sorbet into bowls or glasses and enjoy!

Tips:

- **Pineapple Juice**: Fresh pineapple juice will give the sorbet a more vibrant flavor, but 100% juice from the store works well too.
- **Coconut Milk**: Full-fat coconut milk gives the sorbet a rich, creamy texture. If using light coconut milk, the texture may be less creamy.

- **Rum**: The rum adds a traditional Pina Colada flavor, but it can be omitted for a non-alcoholic version.

Enjoy your homemade Pina Colada Sorbet! It's a tropical, refreshing dessert that brings a taste of the islands right to your home.

Brownie Batter Milkshake

Ingredients

- **1 cup (240ml) whole milk**
- **1/2 cup (120ml) heavy cream**
- **1/2 cup (120g) brownie batter** (see notes for making brownie batter without eggs)
- **2 cups (250g) vanilla ice cream** (or chocolate ice cream for extra richness)
- **1/4 cup (60ml) chocolate syrup** (optional, for extra chocolatey flavor)
- **Whipped cream** (for topping)
- **Chocolate shavings or sprinkles** (for garnish, optional)

Instructions

1. Prepare the Brownie Batter:

1. **Make or Use Store-Bought**: If making from scratch, prepare a small batch of brownie batter without eggs (to avoid raw egg consumption). For store-bought, ensure it's safe to consume raw or use a premade brownie batter that's labeled as safe for raw consumption.
2. **Mix with Milk**: In a bowl, whisk the brownie batter with a little bit of milk to thin it out if needed, making it easier to blend into the milkshake.

2. Blend the Milkshake:

1. **Combine Ingredients**: In a blender, combine the milk, heavy cream, brownie batter, and vanilla ice cream. If using chocolate syrup, add it at this stage.
2. **Blend**: Blend until smooth and creamy. You can adjust the thickness by adding more milk if it's too thick or more ice cream if it's too thin.

3. Serve:

1. **Pour**: Pour the milkshake into a tall glass.
2. **Top**: Top with whipped cream and garnish with chocolate shavings or sprinkles if desired.
3. **Enjoy**: Serve immediately with a straw and enjoy!

Tips:

- **Brownie Batter**: For safety, use a recipe or store-bought batter that is safe to eat raw. You can also use a no-egg brownie batter recipe for this purpose.
- **Ice Cream**: For a richer flavor, use chocolate ice cream instead of vanilla.
- **Milkshake Consistency**: Adjust the thickness of your milkshake by adding more milk for a thinner consistency or more ice cream for a thicker one.

Enjoy your Brownie Batter Milkshake! It's a rich, creamy, and chocolatey indulgence that's perfect for a special treat or a fun dessert.

Cinnamon Roll Ice Cream

Ingredients

For the Ice Cream Base:

- **2 cups (480ml) whole milk**
- **1 cup (240ml) heavy cream**
- **3/4 cup (150g) granulated sugar**
- **4 large egg yolks**
- **1 teaspoon vanilla extract**

For the Cinnamon Roll Swirl:

- **1/2 cup (100g) brown sugar**
- **2 tablespoons ground cinnamon**
- **1/4 cup (60g) unsalted butter**, melted
- **1 cup (250g) cinnamon roll dough** (store-bought or homemade, pre-baked)

Instructions

1. Prepare the Ice Cream Base:

1. **Heat Milk and Cream**: In a medium saucepan, combine the whole milk and heavy cream. Heat over medium heat until the mixture is hot but not boiling.
2. **Whisk Egg Yolks and Sugar**: In a separate bowl, whisk the egg yolks and granulated sugar until light and slightly thickened.
3. **Temper the Egg Yolks**: Gradually add a small amount of the hot milk mixture to the egg yolks, whisking constantly to temper them.
4. **Cook Custard**: Slowly pour the tempered egg yolks back into the saucepan with the remaining milk mixture. Cook over medium heat, stirring constantly, until the mixture thickens and coats the back of a spoon (170°F-175°F or 77°C-80°C). Do not let it boil.
5. **Cool and Chill**: Remove from heat and strain the custard through a fine-mesh sieve into a clean bowl. Stir in the vanilla extract. Let it cool to room temperature, then cover and refrigerate until very cold (at least 4 hours or overnight).

2. Prepare the Cinnamon Roll Swirl:

1. **Make Cinnamon Sugar**: In a small bowl, combine the brown sugar and ground cinnamon.
2. **Prepare Cinnamon Roll Pieces**: If using store-bought cinnamon rolls, bake them according to package instructions and then cut them into small chunks. If using homemade cinnamon rolls, bake them and then chop them into pieces. Allow them to cool.

3. **Mix Cinnamon Sugar and Butter**: Stir the melted butter into the cinnamon sugar mixture to create a cinnamon sugar paste.

3. Churn the Ice Cream:

1. **Churn**: Pour the chilled ice cream base into an ice cream maker and churn according to the manufacturer's instructions, usually about 20-25 minutes, or until it reaches a soft-serve consistency.

4. Swirl in Cinnamon Roll Mixture:

1. **Add Cinnamon Roll Pieces**: When the ice cream is almost done churning, gently fold in the chopped cinnamon roll pieces.
2. **Swirl Cinnamon Sugar**: In a separate bowl, gently swirl the cinnamon sugar paste into the churned ice cream. You can do this by spooning the paste in and gently folding it through, creating a ribbon effect.

5. Freeze:

1. **Firm Up**: Transfer the churned ice cream to an airtight container and freeze for at least 2 hours to firm up.

6. Serve:

1. **Scoop and Enjoy**: Scoop the Cinnamon Roll Ice Cream into bowls or cones and enjoy!

Tips:

- **Cinnamon Rolls**: Use leftover cinnamon rolls or store-bought ones. For the best texture, bake them fresh and allow them to cool before chopping.
- **Swirling**: Gently fold the cinnamon sugar paste into the ice cream to create a swirl effect without fully blending it in.
- **Ice Cream Maker**: Ensure the ice cream maker's bowl is fully frozen before churning for the smoothest texture.

Enjoy your homemade Cinnamon Roll Ice Cream! It's a rich and comforting dessert that combines the best of both ice cream and cinnamon rolls in every bite.

Fig and Honey Gelato

Ingredients

For the Fig Mixture:

- **1 cup (240ml) fresh figs** (or dried figs, if fresh are not available, see note below)
- **1/4 cup (60ml) water**
- **2 tablespoons honey**
- **1 tablespoon lemon juice** (about 1/2 lemon)

For the Gelato Base:

- **2 cups (480ml) whole milk**
- **1 cup (240ml) heavy cream**
- **3/4 cup (150g) granulated sugar**
- **4 large egg yolks**
- **1 teaspoon vanilla extract**

Instructions

1. Prepare the Fig Mixture:

1. **Cook Figs**: If using fresh figs, remove the stems and cut them into quarters. If using dried figs, chop them into small pieces. Place the figs and water in a saucepan and cook over medium heat until the figs are soft and have absorbed most of the water, about 10 minutes.
2. **Blend**: Transfer the cooked figs to a blender or food processor. Add honey and lemon juice. Blend until smooth. Set aside to cool.

2. Prepare the Gelato Base:

1. **Heat Milk and Cream**: In a medium saucepan, combine the whole milk and heavy cream. Heat over medium heat until the mixture is hot but not boiling.
2. **Whisk Egg Yolks and Sugar**: In a separate bowl, whisk the egg yolks and granulated sugar until light and slightly thickened.
3. **Temper the Egg Yolks**: Gradually add a small amount of the hot milk mixture to the egg yolks, whisking constantly to temper them.
4. **Cook Custard**: Slowly pour the tempered egg yolks back into the saucepan with the remaining milk mixture. Cook over medium heat, stirring constantly, until the mixture thickens and coats the back of a spoon (170°F-175°F or 77°C-80°C). Do not let it boil.
5. **Cool and Chill**: Remove from heat and strain the custard through a fine-mesh sieve into a clean bowl. Stir in the vanilla extract. Let it cool to room temperature, then cover and refrigerate until very cold (at least 4 hours or overnight).

3. Combine Fig Mixture and Gelato Base:

1. **Mix Together**: Once the gelato base is chilled, stir in the fig mixture until well combined.

4. Churn the Gelato:

1. **Churn**: Pour the mixture into an ice cream maker and churn according to the manufacturer's instructions, usually about 20-25 minutes, or until it reaches a soft-serve consistency.

5. Freeze:

1. **Firm Up**: Transfer the churned gelato to an airtight container and freeze for at least 2 hours to firm up.

6. Serve:

1. **Scoop and Enjoy**: Scoop the Fig and Honey Gelato into bowls or cones and enjoy!

Tips:

- **Fresh vs. Dried Figs**: If using dried figs, soak them in hot water for about 30 minutes to soften them before cooking. You might need to adjust the water quantity based on how dry the figs are.
- **Sweetness**: Adjust the amount of honey based on your taste preference. The honey can be adjusted if you prefer more or less sweetness.
- **Ice Cream Maker**: Ensure the ice cream maker's bowl is fully frozen before churning for the best texture.

Enjoy your homemade Fig and Honey Gelato! It's a creamy and elegant dessert that highlights the wonderful flavors of figs and honey in a delightful frozen treat.

White Chocolate Raspberry Ice Cream

Ingredients

For the Raspberry Swirl:

- **2 cups (250g) fresh raspberries** (or frozen, thawed)
- **1/2 cup (100g) granulated sugar**
- **1 tablespoon lemon juice** (about 1/2 lemon)

For the Ice Cream Base:

- **2 cups (480ml) whole milk**
- **1 cup (240ml) heavy cream**
- **3/4 cup (150g) granulated sugar**
- **4 large egg yolks**
- **1 cup (170g) white chocolate chips or chopped white chocolate**
- **1 teaspoon vanilla extract**

Instructions

1. Prepare the Raspberry Swirl:

1. **Cook Raspberries**: In a saucepan, combine the raspberries, granulated sugar, and lemon juice. Cook over medium heat, stirring occasionally, until the raspberries break down and the mixture becomes thick and syrupy, about 10 minutes.
2. **Blend and Strain**: Blend the raspberry mixture until smooth, then strain through a fine-mesh sieve to remove seeds. Allow the raspberry sauce to cool to room temperature.

2. Prepare the Ice Cream Base:

1. **Heat Milk and Cream**: In a medium saucepan, combine the whole milk and heavy cream. Heat over medium heat until the mixture is hot but not boiling.
2. **Whisk Egg Yolks and Sugar**: In a separate bowl, whisk the egg yolks and granulated sugar until the mixture is light and slightly thickened.
3. **Temper the Egg Yolks**: Gradually add a small amount of the hot milk mixture to the egg yolks, whisking constantly to temper them.
4. **Cook Custard**: Slowly pour the tempered egg yolks back into the saucepan with the remaining milk mixture. Cook over medium heat, stirring constantly, until the mixture thickens and coats the back of a spoon (170°F-175°F or 77°C-80°C). Do not let it boil.
5. **Add White Chocolate**: Remove from heat and stir in the white chocolate until it is fully melted and incorporated into the custard.

6. **Cool and Chill**: Strain the custard through a fine-mesh sieve into a clean bowl. Stir in the vanilla extract. Let it cool to room temperature, then cover and refrigerate until very cold (at least 4 hours or overnight).

3. Churn the Ice Cream:

1. **Churn**: Pour the chilled ice cream base into an ice cream maker and churn according to the manufacturer's instructions, usually about 20-25 minutes, or until it reaches a soft-serve consistency.

4. Swirl in Raspberry Sauce:

1. **Add Raspberry Swirl**: When the ice cream is almost done churning, gently fold in the raspberry sauce. You can create a swirl effect by gently folding the sauce through the ice cream, leaving ribbons of raspberry throughout.

5. Freeze:

1. **Firm Up**: Transfer the churned ice cream to an airtight container and freeze for at least 2 hours to firm up.

6. Serve:

1. **Scoop and Enjoy**: Scoop the White Chocolate Raspberry Ice Cream into bowls or cones and enjoy!

Tips:

- **White Chocolate**: Use high-quality white chocolate for the best flavor. Chopping it into small pieces helps it melt evenly.
- **Raspberry Sauce**: Adjust the sweetness of the raspberry sauce according to your taste. If you prefer it less sweet, reduce the amount of sugar.
- **Ice Cream Maker**: Ensure the ice cream maker's bowl is fully frozen before churning to achieve the best texture.

Enjoy your homemade White Chocolate Raspberry Ice Cream! It's a creamy, indulgent dessert with a beautiful blend of sweet white chocolate and tart raspberry flavors.

Dulce de Leche Ice Cream

Ingredients

- 1 cup (240ml) whole milk
- 1 cup (240ml) heavy cream
- 3/4 cup (150g) granulated sugar
- 1 cup (240ml) dulce de leche (store-bought or homemade, see note below)
- 4 large egg yolks
- 1 teaspoon vanilla extract

Instructions

1. Prepare the Custard Base:

1. **Heat Milk and Cream**: In a medium saucepan, combine the whole milk and heavy cream. Heat over medium heat until the mixture is hot but not boiling.
2. **Whisk Egg Yolks and Sugar**: In a separate bowl, whisk the egg yolks and granulated sugar until the mixture is light and slightly thickened.
3. **Temper the Egg Yolks**: Gradually add a small amount of the hot milk mixture to the egg yolks, whisking constantly to temper them.
4. **Cook Custard**: Slowly pour the tempered egg yolks back into the saucepan with the remaining milk mixture. Cook over medium heat, stirring constantly, until the mixture thickens and coats the back of a spoon (170°F-175°F or 77°C-80°C). Do not let it boil.
5. **Add Dulce de Leche**: Remove from heat and stir in the dulce de leche until fully combined and smooth.
6. **Cool and Chill**: Strain the custard through a fine-mesh sieve into a clean bowl. Stir in the vanilla extract. Let it cool to room temperature, then cover and refrigerate until very cold (at least 4 hours or overnight).

2. Churn the Ice Cream:

1. **Churn**: Pour the chilled custard base into an ice cream maker and churn according to the manufacturer's instructions, usually about 20-25 minutes, or until it reaches a soft-serve consistency.

3. Freeze:

1. **Firm Up**: Transfer the churned ice cream to an airtight container and freeze for at least 2 hours to firm up.

4. Serve:

1. **Scoop and Enjoy**: Scoop the Dulce de Leche Ice Cream into bowls or cones and enjoy!

Tips:

- **Dulce de Leche**: Use high-quality dulce de leche for the best flavor. You can make it at home by simmering sweetened condensed milk until it turns into a caramel-like consistency.
- **Ice Cream Maker**: Ensure the ice cream maker's bowl is fully frozen before churning for the best texture.
- **Swirls**: For added texture, you can swirl extra dulce de leche into the ice cream during the last few minutes of churning.

Enjoy your homemade Dulce de Leche Ice Cream! It's a creamy and decadent dessert that's sure to satisfy any caramel lover's cravings.

Strawberry-Basil Sorbet

Ingredients

- **4 cups (600g) fresh strawberries**, hulled
- **1 cup (200g) granulated sugar**
- **1/2 cup (120ml) water**
- **1/2 cup (120ml) fresh lemon juice** (about 2 lemons)
- **1/2 cup (packed, about 10-12 large leaves) fresh basil leaves**

Instructions

1. Prepare the Strawberry Mixture:

1. **Blend Strawberries**: In a blender or food processor, blend the hulled strawberries until smooth. Set aside.
2. **Make Simple Syrup**: In a small saucepan, combine the granulated sugar and water. Heat over medium heat, stirring occasionally, until the sugar is fully dissolved. Remove from heat and let cool.
3. **Combine Ingredients**: In a large bowl, combine the blended strawberries, simple syrup, and fresh lemon juice. Stir until well mixed.

2. Infuse the Basil:

1. **Blend Basil**: In a blender or food processor, blend the fresh basil leaves with a small portion of the strawberry mixture (about 1 cup) until smooth.
2. **Mix**: Stir the basil mixture into the rest of the strawberry mixture, ensuring even distribution.

3. Chill the Mixture:

1. **Refrigerate**: Cover the mixture and refrigerate for at least 1 hour to chill thoroughly. This helps the sorbet freeze more evenly.

4. Churn the Sorbet:

1. **Churn**: Pour the chilled mixture into an ice cream maker and churn according to the manufacturer's instructions, usually about 20-25 minutes, or until it reaches a soft-serve consistency.

5. Freeze:

1. **Firm Up**: Transfer the churned sorbet to an airtight container and freeze for at least 2 hours to firm up.

6. Serve:

1. **Scoop and Enjoy**: Scoop the Strawberry-Basil Sorbet into bowls or glasses and enjoy!

Tips:

- **Strawberries**: Use ripe, sweet strawberries for the best flavor. If using frozen strawberries, thaw them before blending.
- **Basil**: Adjust the amount of basil according to your taste preference. If you prefer a subtler basil flavor, start with a smaller amount and adjust as needed.
- **Texture**: If you don't have an ice cream maker, you can freeze the mixture in a shallow dish, stirring every 30 minutes with a fork to break up the ice crystals until it reaches a sorbet-like consistency.

Enjoy your homemade Strawberry-Basil Sorbet! It's a delightful and refreshing treat with a unique twist that's sure to impress.

Carrot Cake Ice Cream

Ingredients

For the Ice Cream Base:

- 2 cups (480ml) whole milk
- 1 cup (240ml) heavy cream
- 3/4 cup (150g) granulated sugar
- 4 large egg yolks
- 1 teaspoon vanilla extract

For the Carrot Cake Mix-Ins:

- **1 cup (120g) finely grated carrots** (about 2 medium carrots)
- **1/2 cup (80g) chopped walnuts** (optional)
- **1/2 cup (80g) raisins** (optional)
- 1 teaspoon ground cinnamon
- 1/2 teaspoon ground nutmeg
- 1/4 teaspoon ground ginger
- 1/4 teaspoon ground cloves

For the Cream Cheese Swirl:

- **1/2 cup (120g) cream cheese**, softened
- 1/4 cup (50g) granulated sugar
- 1/4 cup (60ml) heavy cream
- 1/2 teaspoon vanilla extract

Instructions

1. Prepare the Carrot Cake Mixture:

1. **Cook Carrots**: In a small saucepan, lightly cook the grated carrots with a bit of water until they are tender but not mushy, about 5 minutes. Drain and let cool.
2. **Mix Spices**: In a small bowl, combine the ground cinnamon, nutmeg, ginger, and cloves. Set aside.

2. Prepare the Ice Cream Base:

1. **Heat Milk and Cream**: In a medium saucepan, combine the whole milk and heavy cream. Heat over medium heat until the mixture is hot but not boiling.
2. **Whisk Egg Yolks and Sugar**: In a separate bowl, whisk the egg yolks and granulated sugar until the mixture is light and slightly thickened.
3. **Temper the Egg Yolks**: Gradually add a small amount of the hot milk mixture to the egg yolks, whisking constantly to temper them.

4. **Cook Custard**: Slowly pour the tempered egg yolks back into the saucepan with the remaining milk mixture. Cook over medium heat, stirring constantly, until the mixture thickens and coats the back of a spoon (170°F-175°F or 77°C-80°C). Do not let it boil.
5. **Add Spices**: Remove from heat and stir in the spice mixture. Let the custard cool to room temperature, then cover and refrigerate until very cold (at least 4 hours or overnight).

3. Prepare the Cream Cheese Swirl:

1. **Mix Cream Cheese**: In a bowl, beat together the cream cheese, granulated sugar, heavy cream, and vanilla extract until smooth and creamy.

4. Churn the Ice Cream:

1. **Churn**: Pour the chilled custard base into an ice cream maker and churn according to the manufacturer's instructions, usually about 20-25 minutes, or until it reaches a soft-serve consistency.
2. **Add Carrot Mix-Ins**: Gently fold in the cooked carrots, walnuts, and raisins during the last few minutes of churning.

5. Swirl in Cream Cheese Mixture:

1. **Add Swirl**: Transfer the churned ice cream to an airtight container. Drop spoonfuls of the cream cheese mixture into the ice cream and gently swirl it through with a knife or spoon to create a marbled effect.

6. Freeze:

1. **Firm Up**: Freeze the ice cream for at least 2 hours to firm up.

7. Serve:

1. **Scoop and Enjoy**: Scoop the Carrot Cake Ice Cream into bowls or cones and enjoy!

Tips:

- **Carrots**: Ensure the grated carrots are finely chopped to distribute evenly throughout the ice cream.
- **Cream Cheese Swirl**: For a more pronounced swirl, drop larger spoonfuls of the cream cheese mixture into the ice cream and gently fold.
- **Ice Cream Maker**: Make sure the ice cream maker's bowl is fully frozen before churning for the best texture.

Enjoy your homemade Carrot Cake Ice Cream! It's a creamy and delicious treat that combines the flavors of carrot cake with the cool, refreshing nature of ice cream.

Maple Pecan Gelato

Ingredients

For the Gelato Base:

- 2 cups (480ml) whole milk
- 1 cup (240ml) heavy cream
- 3/4 cup (150g) granulated sugar
- 4 large egg yolks
- 1/2 cup (120ml) pure maple syrup
- 1 teaspoon vanilla extract

For the Pecan Mix-In:

- 1 cup (120g) pecan halves
- 2 tablespoons unsalted butter
- 2 tablespoons maple syrup
- 1/4 teaspoon ground cinnamon (optional)

Instructions

1. Prepare the Pecan Mix-In:

1. **Toast Pecans**: Preheat your oven to 350°F (175°C). Spread the pecan halves on a baking sheet and toast in the oven for about 8-10 minutes, or until fragrant. Watch them closely to prevent burning. Let them cool.
2. **Glaze Pecans**: In a skillet over medium heat, melt the butter. Add the toasted pecans and maple syrup, stirring to coat the pecans evenly. Cook for 2-3 minutes until the syrup thickens slightly. If using, stir in the ground cinnamon. Remove from heat and let cool. Chop the pecans coarsely.

2. Prepare the Gelato Base:

1. **Heat Milk and Cream**: In a medium saucepan, combine the whole milk and heavy cream. Heat over medium heat until the mixture is hot but not boiling.
2. **Whisk Egg Yolks and Sugar**: In a separate bowl, whisk the egg yolks and granulated sugar until the mixture is light and slightly thickened.
3. **Temper the Egg Yolks**: Gradually add a small amount of the hot milk mixture to the egg yolks, whisking constantly to temper them.
4. **Cook Custard**: Slowly pour the tempered egg yolks back into the saucepan with the remaining milk mixture. Cook over medium heat, stirring constantly, until the mixture thickens and coats the back of a spoon (170°F-175°F or 77°C-80°C). Do not let it boil.

5. **Add Maple Syrup**: Remove from heat and stir in the maple syrup and vanilla extract. Let the custard cool to room temperature, then cover and refrigerate until very cold (at least 4 hours or overnight).

3. Churn the Gelato:

1. **Churn**: Pour the chilled custard base into an ice cream maker and churn according to the manufacturer's instructions, usually about 20-25 minutes, or until it reaches a soft-serve consistency.

4. Mix in Pecans:

1. **Add Pecans**: Gently fold the chopped pecans into the churned gelato.

5. Freeze:

1. **Firm Up**: Transfer the gelato to an airtight container and freeze for at least 2 hours to firm up.

6. Serve:

1. **Scoop and Enjoy**: Scoop the Maple Pecan Gelato into bowls or cones and enjoy!

Tips:

- **Maple Syrup**: Use pure maple syrup for the best flavor. Avoid maple-flavored syrups, which are not as rich.
- **Pecans**: Make sure the pecans are cooled before adding them to the gelato. This prevents them from softening the gelato.
- **Ice Cream Maker**: Ensure the ice cream maker's bowl is fully frozen before churning for the best texture.

Enjoy your homemade Maple Pecan Gelato! It's a creamy, indulgent dessert with the perfect balance of sweet maple and crunchy pecans.

Watermelon Mint Sorbet

Ingredients

- **4 cups (600g) seedless watermelon**, cut into chunks
- **1/2 cup (100g) granulated sugar** (adjust to taste based on the sweetness of the watermelon)
- **1/4 cup (60ml) fresh lime juice** (about 2 limes)
- **1/4 cup (60ml) water**
- **1/4 cup (packed, about 8-10 large leaves) fresh mint leaves**

Instructions

1. Prepare the Watermelon:

1. **Blend Watermelon**: In a blender or food processor, blend the watermelon chunks until smooth. Strain through a fine-mesh sieve to remove any pulp if you prefer a smoother texture. You should have about 3 cups of watermelon juice.

2. Prepare the Mint:

1. **Infuse Mint**: In a small saucepan, bring the water to a boil. Add the fresh mint leaves and let them steep for about 5 minutes. Remove from heat and let the mint infusion cool. Strain out the mint leaves.

3. Make the Sorbet Base:

1. **Combine Ingredients**: In a large bowl, combine the watermelon juice, granulated sugar, lime juice, and mint infusion. Stir until the sugar is fully dissolved.

4. Chill the Mixture:

1. **Refrigerate**: Cover the mixture and refrigerate for at least 1 hour to chill thoroughly. This helps the sorbet freeze more evenly.

5. Churn the Sorbet:

1. **Churn**: Pour the chilled mixture into an ice cream maker and churn according to the manufacturer's instructions, usually about 20-25 minutes, or until it reaches a soft-serve consistency.

6. Freeze:

1. **Firm Up**: Transfer the churned sorbet to an airtight container and freeze for at least 2 hours to firm up.

7. Serve:

1. **Scoop and Enjoy**: Scoop the Watermelon Mint Sorbet into bowls or glasses and enjoy!

Tips:

- **Watermelon**: Use ripe, sweet watermelon for the best flavor. If your watermelon is not very sweet, you might need to adjust the amount of sugar.
- **Mint**: If you prefer a stronger mint flavor, you can increase the amount of mint leaves used in the infusion.
- **Ice Cream Maker**: Ensure the ice cream maker's bowl is fully frozen before churning for the best texture.

Enjoy your homemade Watermelon Mint Sorbet! It's a refreshing and flavorful treat that's perfect for cooling off on a warm day.

Hazelnut Coffee Ice Cream

Ingredients

For the Ice Cream Base:

- **2 cups (480ml) whole milk**
- **1 cup (240ml) heavy cream**
- **3/4 cup (150g) granulated sugar**
- **4 large egg yolks**
- **1/2 cup (120ml) brewed strong coffee or espresso** (cooled)
- **1 teaspoon vanilla extract**

For the Hazelnut Mix-In:

- **1 cup (120g) toasted hazelnuts**, chopped
- **1/4 cup (60ml) hazelnut liqueur** (optional, for added flavor)

Instructions

1. Prepare the Hazelnuts:

1. **Toast Hazelnuts**: Preheat your oven to 350°F (175°C). Spread the hazelnuts on a baking sheet and toast in the oven for about 8-10 minutes, or until fragrant and the skins begin to darken. Let cool slightly, then rub the hazelnuts in a clean kitchen towel to remove most of the skins. Chop coarsely.
2. **Optional Step**: If using hazelnut liqueur, toss the chopped hazelnuts with the liqueur and let them sit for about 15 minutes.

2. Prepare the Ice Cream Base:

1. **Heat Milk and Cream**: In a medium saucepan, combine the whole milk and heavy cream. Heat over medium heat until the mixture is hot but not boiling.
2. **Whisk Egg Yolks and Sugar**: In a separate bowl, whisk the egg yolks and granulated sugar until the mixture is light and slightly thickened.
3. **Temper the Egg Yolks**: Gradually add a small amount of the hot milk mixture to the egg yolks, whisking constantly to temper them.
4. **Cook Custard**: Slowly pour the tempered egg yolks back into the saucepan with the remaining milk mixture. Cook over medium heat, stirring constantly, until the mixture thickens and coats the back of a spoon (170°F-175°F or 77°C-80°C). Do not let it boil.
5. **Add Coffee**: Remove from heat and stir in the brewed coffee (or espresso) and vanilla extract. Let the custard cool to room temperature, then cover and refrigerate until very cold (at least 4 hours or overnight).

3. Churn the Ice Cream:

1. **Churn**: Pour the chilled custard base into an ice cream maker and churn according to the manufacturer's instructions, usually about 20-25 minutes, or until it reaches a soft-serve consistency.
2. **Add Hazelnuts**: Gently fold the chopped hazelnuts into the churned ice cream.

4. Freeze:

1. **Firm Up**: Transfer the churned ice cream to an airtight container and freeze for at least 2 hours to firm up.

5. Serve:

1. **Scoop and Enjoy**: Scoop the Hazelnut Coffee Ice Cream into bowls or cones and enjoy!

Tips:

- **Coffee**: Use freshly brewed strong coffee or espresso for the best flavor. If you prefer a stronger coffee flavor, you can adjust the amount used.
- **Hazelnuts**: Toasting the hazelnuts enhances their flavor and gives a pleasant crunch. If you prefer a smoother texture, you can blend some of the hazelnuts into a paste before adding them to the ice cream.
- **Ice Cream Maker**: Make sure the ice cream maker's bowl is fully frozen before churning for the best results.

Enjoy your homemade Hazelnut Coffee Ice Cream! It's a decadent and flavorful dessert that combines the rich taste of coffee with the nutty sweetness of hazelnuts.

Ginger Peach Sorbet

Ingredients

- **4 cups (600g) fresh peaches**, peeled, pitted, and cut into chunks
- **1 cup (200g) granulated sugar**
- **1/4 cup (60ml) fresh lemon juice** (about 2 lemons)
- **1/4 cup (60ml) water**
- **1 tablespoon freshly grated ginger** (adjust to taste)
- **1 teaspoon vanilla extract** (optional)

Instructions

1. Prepare the Peaches:

1. **Blend Peaches**: In a blender or food processor, blend the peach chunks until smooth. If you prefer a smoother sorbet, strain the peach puree through a fine-mesh sieve to remove any pulp. You should have about 3 cups of peach puree.

2. Prepare the Ginger Syrup:

1. **Cook Syrup**: In a small saucepan, combine the water and granulated sugar. Heat over medium heat, stirring occasionally, until the sugar is fully dissolved. Remove from heat and stir in the freshly grated ginger. Let it steep for about 5 minutes, then strain out the ginger pieces.

3. Make the Sorbet Base:

1. **Combine Ingredients**: In a large bowl, combine the peach puree, ginger syrup, and fresh lemon juice. Stir until well mixed. If using vanilla extract, add it here.

4. Chill the Mixture:

1. **Refrigerate**: Cover the mixture and refrigerate for at least 1 hour to chill thoroughly. This helps the sorbet freeze more evenly.

5. Churn the Sorbet:

1. **Churn**: Pour the chilled mixture into an ice cream maker and churn according to the manufacturer's instructions, usually about 20-25 minutes, or until it reaches a soft-serve consistency.

6. Freeze:

1. **Firm Up**: Transfer the churned sorbet to an airtight container and freeze for at least 2 hours to firm up.

7. Serve:

1. **Scoop and Enjoy**: Scoop the Ginger Peach Sorbet into bowls or glasses and enjoy!

Tips:

- **Peaches**: Use ripe, sweet peaches for the best flavor. If peaches are not in season, you can use frozen peaches, but make sure they are thawed before blending.
- **Ginger**: Adjust the amount of ginger based on your preference. Fresh ginger adds a nice spicy kick, but you can use less if you prefer a subtler flavor.
- **Ice Cream Maker**: Ensure the ice cream maker's bowl is fully frozen before churning for the best texture.

Enjoy your homemade Ginger Peach Sorbet! It's a refreshing and flavorful treat that perfectly balances the sweetness of peaches with the warmth of ginger.

Vanilla Espresso Gelato

Ingredients

For the Gelato Base:

- **2 cups (480ml) whole milk**
- **1 cup (240ml) heavy cream**
- **3/4 cup (150g) granulated sugar**
- **4 large egg yolks**
- **1 tablespoon vanilla extract**
- **1/2 cup (120ml) strong brewed espresso** (cooled)

Instructions

1. Prepare the Gelato Base:

1. **Heat Milk and Cream**: In a medium saucepan, combine the whole milk and heavy cream. Heat over medium heat until the mixture is hot but not boiling.
2. **Whisk Egg Yolks and Sugar**: In a separate bowl, whisk the egg yolks and granulated sugar until the mixture is light and slightly thickened.
3. **Temper the Egg Yolks**: Gradually add a small amount of the hot milk mixture to the egg yolks, whisking constantly to temper them.
4. **Cook Custard**: Slowly pour the tempered egg yolks back into the saucepan with the remaining milk mixture. Cook over medium heat, stirring constantly, until the mixture thickens and coats the back of a spoon (170°F-175°F or 77°C-80°C). Do not let it boil.
5. **Add Vanilla and Espresso**: Remove from heat and stir in the vanilla extract and brewed espresso. Mix until fully combined. Let the custard cool to room temperature, then cover and refrigerate until very cold (at least 4 hours or overnight).

2. Churn the Gelato:

1. **Churn**: Pour the chilled custard base into an ice cream maker and churn according to the manufacturer's instructions, usually about 20-25 minutes, or until it reaches a soft-serve consistency.

3. Freeze:

1. **Firm Up**: Transfer the churned gelato to an airtight container and freeze for at least 2 hours to firm up.

4. Serve:

1. **Scoop and Enjoy**: Scoop the Vanilla Espresso Gelato into bowls or cones and enjoy!

Tips:

- **Espresso**: Use freshly brewed espresso for the best flavor. If you don't have an espresso machine, you can use strong brewed coffee as a substitute.
- **Gelato Texture**: Gelato is typically denser and creamier than ice cream. If you want an extra-smooth texture, make sure the ice cream maker's bowl is fully frozen before churning.
- **Vanilla Extract**: Use pure vanilla extract for the best flavor.

Enjoy your homemade Vanilla Espresso Gelato! It's a luxurious and creamy dessert with a delightful coffee kick and a smooth vanilla finish.

Cherry Almond Ice Cream

Ingredients

For the Ice Cream Base:

- **2 cups (480ml) whole milk**
- **1 cup (240ml) heavy cream**
- **3/4 cup (150g) granulated sugar**
- **4 large egg yolks**
- **1 teaspoon vanilla extract**
- **1/2 teaspoon almond extract**

For the Cherry Mix-In:

- **2 cups (300g) fresh or frozen cherries**, pitted and chopped (if using frozen, thaw and drain them)
- **1/4 cup (50g) granulated sugar**
- **1 tablespoon lemon juice**
- **1/2 cup (60g) chopped almonds** (toasted or raw, according to preference)

Instructions

1. Prepare the Cherry Mixture:

1. **Cook Cherries**: In a medium saucepan, combine the chopped cherries, granulated sugar, and lemon juice. Cook over medium heat for about 5-7 minutes, stirring occasionally, until the cherries release their juices and the mixture thickens slightly. Let it cool to room temperature.
2. **Chop Almonds**: If not already chopped, chop the almonds to your desired size. Toasting them is optional but adds extra flavor. To toast, spread the almonds on a baking sheet and bake at 350°F (175°C) for 8-10 minutes, stirring occasionally, until fragrant and golden. Let them cool.

2. Prepare the Ice Cream Base:

1. **Heat Milk and Cream**: In a medium saucepan, combine the whole milk and heavy cream. Heat over medium heat until the mixture is hot but not boiling.
2. **Whisk Egg Yolks and Sugar**: In a separate bowl, whisk the egg yolks and granulated sugar until the mixture is light and slightly thickened.
3. **Temper the Egg Yolks**: Gradually add a small amount of the hot milk mixture to the egg yolks, whisking constantly to temper them.
4. **Cook Custard**: Slowly pour the tempered egg yolks back into the saucepan with the remaining milk mixture. Cook over medium heat, stirring constantly, until the mixture thickens and coats the back of a spoon (170°F-175°F or 77°C-80°C). Do not let it boil.

5. **Add Flavors**: Remove from heat and stir in the vanilla extract and almond extract. Let the custard cool to room temperature, then cover and refrigerate until very cold (at least 4 hours or overnight).

3. Churn the Ice Cream:

1. **Churn**: Pour the chilled custard base into an ice cream maker and churn according to the manufacturer's instructions, usually about 20-25 minutes, or until it reaches a soft-serve consistency.
2. **Add Cherries and Almonds**: During the last few minutes of churning, gently fold in the cherry mixture and chopped almonds.

4. Freeze:

1. **Firm Up**: Transfer the churned ice cream to an airtight container and freeze for at least 2 hours to firm up.

5. Serve:

1. **Scoop and Enjoy**: Scoop the Cherry Almond Ice Cream into bowls or cones and enjoy!

Tips:

- **Cherries**: If using fresh cherries, make sure they are ripe and sweet. If using frozen cherries, make sure they are well-drained to prevent excess water in the ice cream.
- **Almonds**: Toasting the almonds enhances their flavor, but raw almonds work fine too. Adjust the quantity based on your preference for nutty texture.
- **Ice Cream Maker**: Ensure the ice cream maker's bowl is fully frozen before churning for the best texture.

Enjoy your homemade Cherry Almond Ice Cream! It's a creamy and delightful treat with a wonderful blend of fruity and nutty flavors.

Tiramisu Gelato

Ingredients

For the Gelato Base:

- **2 cups (480ml) whole milk**
- **1 cup (240ml) heavy cream**
- **3/4 cup (150g) granulated sugar**
- **4 large egg yolks**
- **1/2 cup (120ml) strong brewed espresso** (cooled)
- **1/2 cup (120g) mascarpone cheese**
- **1 teaspoon vanilla extract**

For the Coffee Soak:

- **1/2 cup (120ml) strong brewed coffee or espresso** (cooled)
- **2 tablespoons coffee liqueur** (optional, such as Kahlúa) or 1 tablespoon sugar for a non-alcoholic version

For the Cocoa Swirl:

- **2 tablespoons unsweetened cocoa powder**
- **1 tablespoon granulated sugar**
- **1/4 cup (60ml) heavy cream**

Instructions

1. Prepare the Gelato Base:

1. **Heat Milk and Cream**: In a medium saucepan, combine the whole milk and heavy cream. Heat over medium heat until the mixture is hot but not boiling.
2. **Whisk Egg Yolks and Sugar**: In a separate bowl, whisk the egg yolks and granulated sugar until the mixture is light and slightly thickened.
3. **Temper the Egg Yolks**: Gradually add a small amount of the hot milk mixture to the egg yolks, whisking constantly to temper them.
4. **Cook Custard**: Slowly pour the tempered egg yolks back into the saucepan with the remaining milk mixture. Cook over medium heat, stirring constantly, until the mixture thickens and coats the back of a spoon (170°F-175°F or 77°C-80°C). Do not let it boil.
5. **Add Flavors**: Remove from heat and stir in the brewed espresso, mascarpone cheese, and vanilla extract. Mix until the mascarpone is fully incorporated and the custard is smooth. Let the custard cool to room temperature, then cover and refrigerate until very cold (at least 4 hours or overnight).

2. Prepare the Coffee Soak:

1. **Mix Soak**: In a small bowl, combine the cooled brewed coffee or espresso with the coffee liqueur (if using) or granulated sugar. Stir to combine.

3. Prepare the Cocoa Swirl:

1. **Make Cocoa Mixture**: In a small saucepan, whisk together the cocoa powder, granulated sugar, and heavy cream. Heat over medium heat, stirring constantly, until the mixture is smooth and slightly thickened. Remove from heat and let it cool.

4. Churn the Gelato:

1. **Churn**: Pour the chilled custard base into an ice cream maker and churn according to the manufacturer's instructions, usually about 20-25 minutes, or until it reaches a soft-serve consistency.
2. **Add Coffee Soak**: During the last few minutes of churning, drizzle the coffee soak over the gelato to create a swirl effect. Do not overmix; you want to have ribbons of coffee flavor throughout.
3. **Swirl Cocoa Mixture**: Gently fold the cooled cocoa mixture into the churned gelato to create a marbled effect.

5. Freeze:

1. **Firm Up**: Transfer the churned gelato to an airtight container and freeze for at least 2 hours to firm up.

6. Serve:

1. **Scoop and Enjoy**: Scoop the Tiramisu Gelato into bowls or cones and enjoy!

Tips:

- **Espresso**: Use freshly brewed espresso or strong coffee for the best flavor. If you don't have an espresso machine, make a strong coffee and let it cool.
- **Mascarpone Cheese**: Ensure the mascarpone cheese is at room temperature before adding it to the custard base for easier blending.
- **Ice Cream Maker**: Make sure the ice cream maker's bowl is fully frozen before churning for the best texture.

Enjoy your homemade Tiramisu Gelato! It's a luxurious and creamy dessert with the delightful flavors of coffee, cocoa, and mascarpone.

Apple Pie Sorbet

Ingredients

- **4 cups (600g) apples**, peeled, cored, and chopped (about 4 medium apples)
- **1 cup (200g) granulated sugar**
- **1/2 cup (120ml) water**
- **1 tablespoon lemon juice** (about 1 lemon)
- **1 teaspoon ground cinnamon**
- **1/4 teaspoon ground nutmeg**
- **1/4 teaspoon ground ginger**
- **1/4 teaspoon salt**
- **1/2 teaspoon vanilla extract**

Instructions

1. Prepare the Apples:

1. **Cook Apples**: In a medium saucepan, combine the chopped apples, granulated sugar, and water. Cook over medium heat, stirring occasionally, until the apples are tender and the mixture has thickened slightly, about 10-15 minutes.
2. **Add Spices**: Stir in the ground cinnamon, ground nutmeg, ground ginger, and salt. Cook for an additional 2 minutes, then remove from heat.
3. **Cool Apples**: Allow the apple mixture to cool to room temperature.

2. Blend the Mixture:

1. **Blend**: Transfer the cooled apple mixture to a blender or food processor and blend until smooth. You should have about 3 cups of apple puree.
2. **Add Lemon Juice and Vanilla**: Stir in the lemon juice and vanilla extract.

3. Chill the Mixture:

1. **Refrigerate**: Cover the apple mixture and refrigerate for at least 1 hour to chill thoroughly. This helps the sorbet freeze more evenly.

4. Churn the Sorbet:

1. **Churn**: Pour the chilled apple mixture into an ice cream maker and churn according to the manufacturer's instructions, usually about 20-25 minutes, or until it reaches a soft-serve consistency.

5. Freeze:

1. **Firm Up**: Transfer the churned sorbet to an airtight container and freeze for at least 2 hours to firm up.

6. Serve:

1. **Scoop and Enjoy**: Scoop the Apple Pie Sorbet into bowls or glasses and enjoy!

Tips:

- **Apples**: Use a variety of apples for a balanced flavor. Honeycrisp, Granny Smith, or Fuji apples work well.
- **Texture**: If you prefer a smoother texture, you can strain the apple puree through a fine-mesh sieve to remove any remaining bits of apple.
- **Ice Cream Maker**: Ensure the ice cream maker's bowl is fully frozen before churning for the best texture.

Enjoy your homemade Apple Pie Sorbet! It's a delicious and refreshing dessert that captures the comforting flavors of apple pie in a light, fruity sorbet.

Coconut Almond Ice Cream

Ingredients

For the Ice Cream Base:

- **2 cups (480ml) coconut milk** (full-fat for creaminess)
- **1 cup (240ml) heavy cream**
- **3/4 cup (150g) granulated sugar**
- **4 large egg yolks**
- **1 teaspoon vanilla extract**
- **1/2 teaspoon almond extract**

For the Almond Mix-In:

- **1 cup (120g) toasted almonds**, chopped
- **1/4 cup (60ml) almond liqueur** (optional, such as Amaretto) or 1 tablespoon sugar for a non-alcoholic version

Instructions

1. Prepare the Almonds:

1. **Toast Almonds**: Preheat your oven to 350°F (175°C). Spread the almonds on a baking sheet and toast in the oven for about 8-10 minutes, or until fragrant and golden brown. Let them cool slightly, then chop coarsely. If using almond liqueur, toss the chopped almonds with it and let them sit for about 15 minutes.

2. Prepare the Ice Cream Base:

1. **Heat Coconut Milk and Cream**: In a medium saucepan, combine the coconut milk and heavy cream. Heat over medium heat until the mixture is hot but not boiling.
2. **Whisk Egg Yolks and Sugar**: In a separate bowl, whisk the egg yolks and granulated sugar until the mixture is light and slightly thickened.
3. **Temper the Egg Yolks**: Gradually add a small amount of the hot coconut mixture to the egg yolks, whisking constantly to temper them.
4. **Cook Custard**: Slowly pour the tempered egg yolks back into the saucepan with the remaining coconut mixture. Cook over medium heat, stirring constantly, until the mixture thickens and coats the back of a spoon (170°F-175°F or 77°C-80°C). Do not let it boil.
5. **Add Flavors**: Remove from heat and stir in the vanilla extract and almond extract. Let the custard cool to room temperature, then cover and refrigerate until very cold (at least 4 hours or overnight).

3. Churn the Ice Cream:

1. **Churn**: Pour the chilled custard base into an ice cream maker and churn according to the manufacturer's instructions, usually about 20-25 minutes, or until it reaches a soft-serve consistency.
2. **Add Almonds**: During the last few minutes of churning, gently fold in the chopped toasted almonds.

4. Freeze:

1. **Firm Up**: Transfer the churned ice cream to an airtight container and freeze for at least 2 hours to firm up.

5. Serve:

1. **Scoop and Enjoy**: Scoop the Coconut Almond Ice Cream into bowls or cones and enjoy!

Tips:

- **Coconut Milk**: Use full-fat coconut milk for a richer, creamier texture. Light coconut milk can be used, but the texture might be less creamy.
- **Almonds**: Toasting the almonds enhances their flavor and gives a pleasant crunch. Adjust the quantity based on your preference for nutty texture.
- **Ice Cream Maker**: Make sure the ice cream maker's bowl is fully frozen before churning for the best texture.

Enjoy your homemade Coconut Almond Ice Cream! It's a creamy, nutty, and tropical dessert that's perfect for a summer day or as a special treat.

Key Lime Pie Gelato

Ingredients

For the Gelato Base:

- 2 cups (480ml) whole milk
- 1 cup (240ml) heavy cream
- 3/4 cup (150g) granulated sugar
- 4 large egg yolks
- 1/2 cup (120ml) fresh key lime juice (or regular lime juice if key limes are unavailable)
- 1 tablespoon lime zest (from about 2 limes)
- 1 teaspoon vanilla extract

For the Graham Cracker Swirl:

- 1 cup (100g) graham cracker crumbs
- 1/4 cup (50g) granulated sugar
- 2 tablespoons unsalted butter, melted

Instructions

1. Prepare the Graham Cracker Swirl:

1. **Combine Ingredients**: In a bowl, mix the graham cracker crumbs, granulated sugar, and melted butter until the crumbs are evenly coated.
2. **Bake**: Spread the mixture on a baking sheet and bake at 350°F (175°C) for about 8-10 minutes, stirring once halfway through, until golden and crispy. Let it cool to room temperature.

2. Prepare the Gelato Base:

1. **Heat Milk and Cream**: In a medium saucepan, combine the whole milk and heavy cream. Heat over medium heat until the mixture is hot but not boiling.
2. **Whisk Egg Yolks and Sugar**: In a separate bowl, whisk the egg yolks and granulated sugar until the mixture is light and slightly thickened.
3. **Temper the Egg Yolks**: Gradually add a small amount of the hot milk mixture to the egg yolks, whisking constantly to temper them.
4. **Cook Custard**: Slowly pour the tempered egg yolks back into the saucepan with the remaining milk mixture. Cook over medium heat, stirring constantly, until the mixture thickens and coats the back of a spoon (170°F-175°F or 77°C-80°C). Do not let it boil.
5. **Add Lime Flavor**: Remove from heat and stir in the fresh lime juice, lime zest, and vanilla extract. Mix until well combined. Let the custard cool to room temperature, then cover and refrigerate until very cold (at least 4 hours or overnight).

3. Churn the Gelato:

1. **Churn**: Pour the chilled custard base into an ice cream maker and churn according to the manufacturer's instructions, usually about 20-25 minutes, or until it reaches a soft-serve consistency.
2. **Add Graham Cracker Swirl**: During the last few minutes of churning, gently fold in the graham cracker crumbs, leaving some chunks for texture.

4. Freeze:

1. **Firm Up**: Transfer the churned gelato to an airtight container and freeze for at least 2 hours to firm up.

5. Serve:

1. **Scoop and Enjoy**: Scoop the Key Lime Pie Gelato into bowls or cones and enjoy!

Tips:

- **Key Limes**: If you can't find key limes, regular limes work perfectly well. Adjust the amount of juice to taste.
- **Graham Cracker Crumbs**: Ensure the graham cracker crumbs are cooled before adding them to the gelato to maintain their crunch.
- **Ice Cream Maker**: Ensure the ice cream maker's bowl is fully frozen before churning for the best texture.

Enjoy your homemade Key Lime Pie Gelato! It's a creamy, tangy dessert with the delightful crunch of graham crackers, perfect for a refreshing treat.

Berry Cheesecake Sorbet

Ingredients

For the Berry Puree:

- **4 cups (600g) mixed berries** (such as strawberries, blueberries, raspberries, and blackberries)
- **1/2 cup (100g) granulated sugar**
- **1 tablespoon lemon juice** (about 1 lemon)

For the Cheesecake Mixture:

- **1 cup (240ml) whole milk**
- **1 cup (240ml) heavy cream**
- **1/2 cup (120g) cream cheese**, softened
- **1/2 cup (100g) granulated sugar**
- **1 teaspoon vanilla extract**
- **1 tablespoon lemon juice** (about 1 lemon)

Instructions

1. Prepare the Berry Puree:

1. **Cook Berries**: In a medium saucepan, combine the mixed berries, granulated sugar, and lemon juice. Cook over medium heat, stirring occasionally, until the berries are soft and the mixture has thickened slightly, about 10-15 minutes.
2. **Blend**: Transfer the cooked berries to a blender or food processor and blend until smooth. Strain the puree through a fine-mesh sieve to remove seeds and pulp, if desired. Let the berry puree cool to room temperature.

2. Prepare the Cheesecake Mixture:

1. **Blend Ingredients**: In a blender or food processor, combine the whole milk, heavy cream, cream cheese, granulated sugar, vanilla extract, and lemon juice. Blend until smooth and the cream cheese is fully incorporated.

3. Combine Berry and Cheesecake Mixtures:

1. **Mix**: In a large bowl, combine the berry puree and the cheesecake mixture. Stir well to ensure the mixtures are fully combined.

4. Chill the Mixture:

1. **Refrigerate**: Cover the mixture and refrigerate for at least 2 hours to chill thoroughly. This helps the sorbet freeze more evenly.

5. Churn the Sorbet:

1. **Churn**: Pour the chilled mixture into an ice cream maker and churn according to the manufacturer's instructions, usually about 20-25 minutes, or until it reaches a soft-serve consistency.

6. Freeze:

1. **Firm Up**: Transfer the churned sorbet to an airtight container and freeze for at least 2 hours to firm up.

7. Serve:

1. **Scoop and Enjoy**: Scoop the Berry Cheesecake Sorbet into bowls or glasses and enjoy!

Tips:

- **Berry Mix**: You can use fresh or frozen berries. If using frozen, thaw and drain them before cooking.
- **Cheese Texture**: Ensure the cream cheese is softened for easier blending and smooth texture.
- **Sweetness**: Adjust the sweetness of the berry puree and cheesecake mixture to your taste. You can add more sugar if needed.

Enjoy your homemade Berry Cheesecake Sorbet! It's a creamy, fruity, and refreshing dessert that combines the best of cheesecake and sorbet in every bite.

Spiced Pear Ice Cream

Ingredients

For the Pear Mixture:

- **4 large ripe pears**, peeled, cored, and chopped
- **1/2 cup (100g) granulated sugar**
- **1 tablespoon lemon juice** (about 1 lemon)
- **1/2 teaspoon ground cinnamon**
- **1/4 teaspoon ground nutmeg**
- **1/4 teaspoon ground ginger**

For the Ice Cream Base:

- **2 cups (480ml) whole milk**
- **1 cup (240ml) heavy cream**
- **3/4 cup (150g) granulated sugar**
- **4 large egg yolks**
- **1 teaspoon vanilla extract**

Instructions

1. Prepare the Pear Mixture:

1. **Cook Pears**: In a medium saucepan, combine the chopped pears, granulated sugar, lemon juice, ground cinnamon, ground nutmeg, and ground ginger. Cook over medium heat, stirring occasionally, until the pears are tender and the mixture is thickened, about 10-15 minutes.
2. **Blend**: Transfer the pear mixture to a blender or food processor and blend until smooth. Let the pear puree cool to room temperature.

2. Prepare the Ice Cream Base:

1. **Heat Milk and Cream**: In a medium saucepan, combine the whole milk and heavy cream. Heat over medium heat until the mixture is hot but not boiling.
2. **Whisk Egg Yolks and Sugar**: In a separate bowl, whisk the egg yolks and granulated sugar until the mixture is light and slightly thickened.
3. **Temper the Egg Yolks**: Gradually add a small amount of the hot milk mixture to the egg yolks, whisking constantly to temper them.
4. **Cook Custard**: Slowly pour the tempered egg yolks back into the saucepan with the remaining milk mixture. Cook over medium heat, stirring constantly, until the mixture thickens and coats the back of a spoon (170°F-175°F or 77°C-80°C). Do not let it boil.

5. **Add Vanilla**: Remove from heat and stir in the vanilla extract. Let the custard cool to room temperature, then cover and refrigerate until very cold (at least 4 hours or overnight).

3. Combine Pear Puree and Custard:

1. **Mix**: Once the custard base is fully chilled, combine it with the pear puree in a large bowl. Stir well to ensure the mixture is fully combined.

4. Churn the Ice Cream:

1. **Churn**: Pour the mixture into an ice cream maker and churn according to the manufacturer's instructions, usually about 20-25 minutes, or until it reaches a soft-serve consistency.

5. Freeze:

1. **Firm Up**: Transfer the churned ice cream to an airtight container and freeze for at least 2 hours to firm up.

6. Serve:

1. **Scoop and Enjoy**: Scoop the Spiced Pear Ice Cream into bowls or cones and enjoy!

Tips:

- **Pears**: Use ripe pears for the best flavor. Bartlett or Anjou pears are good choices.
- **Spices**: Adjust the spices according to your preference. You can add a pinch of cloves or allspice for additional warmth.
- **Ice Cream Maker**: Make sure the ice cream maker's bowl is fully frozen before churning for the best texture.

Enjoy your homemade Spiced Pear Ice Cream! It's a creamy, spiced treat that perfectly combines the sweetness of pears with aromatic spices.

Chocolate Peanut Butter Swirl

Ingredients

For the Chocolate Ice Cream Base:

- **2 cups (480ml) whole milk**
- **1 cup (240ml) heavy cream**
- **3/4 cup (150g) granulated sugar**
- **1/2 cup (45g) unsweetened cocoa powder**
- **4 large egg yolks**
- **1 teaspoon vanilla extract**

For the Peanut Butter Swirl:

- **1/2 cup (120g) creamy peanut butter**
- **1/4 cup (60ml) heavy cream**
- **1/4 cup (50g) granulated sugar**
- **1 tablespoon light corn syrup** (optional, for smoother texture)

Instructions

1. Prepare the Chocolate Ice Cream Base:

1. **Heat Milk and Cream**: In a medium saucepan, combine the whole milk, heavy cream, and granulated sugar. Heat over medium heat until the mixture is hot but not boiling.
2. **Mix Cocoa Powder**: In a small bowl, whisk the unsweetened cocoa powder with a few tablespoons of hot milk mixture until smooth. Add this cocoa mixture back to the saucepan and whisk to combine. Continue to heat until the mixture is hot.
3. **Whisk Egg Yolks**: In a separate bowl, whisk the egg yolks until light and slightly thickened.
4. **Temper the Egg Yolks**: Gradually add a small amount of the hot milk mixture to the egg yolks, whisking constantly to temper them.
5. **Cook Custard**: Slowly pour the tempered egg yolks back into the saucepan with the remaining hot milk mixture. Cook over medium heat, stirring constantly, until the mixture thickens and coats the back of a spoon (170°F-175°F or 77°C-80°C). Do not let it boil.
6. **Add Vanilla**: Remove from heat and stir in the vanilla extract. Let the custard cool to room temperature, then cover and refrigerate until very cold (at least 4 hours or overnight).

2. Prepare the Peanut Butter Swirl:

1. **Mix Peanut Butter**: In a small saucepan, combine the creamy peanut butter, heavy cream, granulated sugar, and light corn syrup (if using). Heat over low heat, stirring constantly, until the mixture is smooth and well combined. Let it cool slightly.

3. Churn the Chocolate Ice Cream:

1. **Churn**: Pour the chilled chocolate custard into an ice cream maker and churn according to the manufacturer's instructions, usually about 20-25 minutes, or until it reaches a soft-serve consistency.

4. Swirl in Peanut Butter:

1. **Layer and Swirl**: Transfer the churned chocolate ice cream to an airtight container. Drop spoonfuls of the peanut butter mixture over the top of the ice cream and use a knife or skewer to gently swirl the peanut butter into the chocolate ice cream. Be careful not to over-mix; you want distinct ribbons of peanut butter throughout.

5. Freeze:

1. **Firm Up**: Freeze the ice cream for at least 2 hours to firm up before serving.

6. Serve:

1. **Scoop and Enjoy**: Scoop the Chocolate Peanut Butter Swirl Ice Cream into bowls or cones and enjoy!

Tips:

- **Peanut Butter**: Use creamy peanut butter for a smooth swirl. If you prefer crunchy, you can use that, but it may not swirl as smoothly.
- **Corn Syrup**: Light corn syrup helps keep the peanut butter swirl smooth and easy to mix. It's optional but recommended for a better texture.
- **Ice Cream Maker**: Ensure the ice cream maker's bowl is fully frozen before churning for the best texture.

Enjoy your homemade Chocolate Peanut Butter Swirl Ice Cream! It's a rich, creamy, and irresistible treat that combines two classic flavors in every bite.

Hibiscus Lime Sorbet

Ingredients

For the Hibiscus Lime Sorbet:

- **1/2 cup (50g) dried hibiscus flowers** (also known as hibiscus tea or hibiscus petals)
- **1 cup (240ml) water**
- **1 cup (200g) granulated sugar**
- **1 cup (240ml) fresh lime juice** (about 6-8 limes)
- **1 tablespoon lime zest** (from about 2 limes)
- **1/2 cup (120ml) water** (for the hibiscus infusion)
- **1/4 teaspoon salt**

Instructions

1. Prepare the Hibiscus Infusion:

1. **Boil Water**: In a medium saucepan, bring 1 cup (240ml) of water to a boil.
2. **Steep Hibiscus Flowers**: Add the dried hibiscus flowers to the boiling water. Remove from heat, cover, and let steep for 10-15 minutes.
3. **Strain**: Strain the hibiscus tea through a fine-mesh sieve into a bowl, discarding the solids. Let the liquid cool to room temperature.

2. Prepare the Sorbet Mixture:

1. **Combine Ingredients**: In a large bowl, combine the hibiscus infusion, granulated sugar, fresh lime juice, lime zest, and salt. Stir until the sugar is fully dissolved.
2. **Chill**: Cover the mixture and refrigerate for at least 1 hour to chill thoroughly. This helps the sorbet freeze more evenly.

3. Churn the Sorbet:

1. **Churn**: Pour the chilled mixture into an ice cream maker and churn according to the manufacturer's instructions, usually about 20-25 minutes, or until it reaches a slushy, sorbet-like consistency.

4. Freeze:

1. **Firm Up**: Transfer the churned sorbet to an airtight container and freeze for at least 2 hours to firm up.

5. Serve:

1. **Scoop and Enjoy**: Scoop the Hibiscus Lime Sorbet into bowls or glasses and enjoy!

Tips:

- **Hibiscus Flowers**: If you can't find dried hibiscus flowers, you can use hibiscus tea bags. Use 2-3 bags, steeped in 1 cup of boiling water.
- **Lime Juice**: Fresh lime juice is preferred for the best flavor, but bottled juice can be used in a pinch.
- **Sweetness**: Adjust the amount of sugar based on your taste and the tartness of the limes.

Enjoy your homemade Hibiscus Lime Sorbet! It's a beautifully vibrant and refreshing dessert that offers a unique and delightful twist on traditional sorbets.

Banana Cream Pie Ice Cream

Ingredients

For the Banana Ice Cream Base:

- **2 cups (480ml) whole milk**
- **1 cup (240ml) heavy cream**
- **3/4 cup (150g) granulated sugar**
- **1/2 cup (120g) ripe banana puree** (about 2 ripe bananas, mashed and blended)
- **4 large egg yolks**
- **1 teaspoon vanilla extract**
- **1/4 teaspoon ground cinnamon** (optional, for added flavor)

For the Graham Cracker Crust Swirl:

- **1 cup (100g) graham cracker crumbs**
- **1/4 cup (50g) granulated sugar**
- **2 tablespoons unsalted butter**, melted

Instructions

1. Prepare the Graham Cracker Crust:

1. **Combine Ingredients**: In a bowl, mix the graham cracker crumbs, granulated sugar, and melted butter until the crumbs are evenly coated.
2. **Bake**: Spread the mixture on a baking sheet and bake at 350°F (175°C) for about 8-10 minutes, stirring once halfway through, until golden and crispy. Let it cool to room temperature.

2. Prepare the Banana Ice Cream Base:

1. **Heat Milk and Cream**: In a medium saucepan, combine the whole milk and heavy cream. Heat over medium heat until the mixture is hot but not boiling.
2. **Whisk Egg Yolks and Sugar**: In a separate bowl, whisk the egg yolks and granulated sugar until the mixture is light and slightly thickened.
3. **Temper the Egg Yolks**: Gradually add a small amount of the hot milk mixture to the egg yolks, whisking constantly to temper them.
4. **Cook Custard**: Slowly pour the tempered egg yolks back into the saucepan with the remaining milk mixture. Cook over medium heat, stirring constantly, until the mixture thickens and coats the back of a spoon (170°F-175°F or 77°C-80°C). Do not let it boil.
5. **Add Banana Puree and Vanilla**: Remove from heat and stir in the banana puree, vanilla extract, and ground cinnamon (if using). Mix until well combined. Let the custard cool to room temperature, then cover and refrigerate until very cold (at least 4 hours or overnight).

3. Churn the Ice Cream:

1. **Churn**: Pour the chilled banana custard into an ice cream maker and churn according to the manufacturer's instructions, usually about 20-25 minutes, or until it reaches a soft-serve consistency.
2. **Add Graham Cracker Crust**: During the last few minutes of churning, gently fold in the graham cracker crumbs, leaving some chunks for texture.

4. Freeze:

1. **Firm Up**: Transfer the churned ice cream to an airtight container and freeze for at least 2 hours to firm up.

5. Serve:

1. **Scoop and Enjoy**: Scoop the Banana Cream Pie Ice Cream into bowls or cones and enjoy!

Tips:

- **Banana Puree**: Ensure the bananas are very ripe for the best flavor. Blend until smooth to avoid any chunks.
- **Graham Cracker Crumbs**: To keep the crumbs from getting too soggy, add them at the end of churning or just before transferring the ice cream to the freezer.
- **Ice Cream Maker**: Ensure the ice cream maker's bowl is fully frozen before churning for the best texture.

Enjoy your homemade Banana Cream Pie Ice Cream! It's a creamy and indulgent treat that brings the classic dessert flavors into a cool and refreshing frozen form.

Pomegranate Sorbet

Ingredients

- **2 cups (480ml) pomegranate juice** (fresh or store-bought)
- **1 cup (200g) granulated sugar**
- **1/2 cup (120ml) water**
- **1 tablespoon lemon juice** (about 1 lemon)
- **1/4 teaspoon salt**

Instructions

1. Prepare the Simple Syrup:

1. **Combine Ingredients**: In a small saucepan, combine the water and granulated sugar.
2. **Heat**: Heat over medium heat, stirring constantly, until the sugar is fully dissolved and the mixture is clear. This usually takes about 3-5 minutes.
3. **Cool**: Remove from heat and let the simple syrup cool to room temperature.

2. Combine Ingredients:

1. **Mix**: In a large bowl, combine the pomegranate juice, cooled simple syrup, lemon juice, and salt. Stir until well combined.

3. Chill the Mixture:

1. **Refrigerate**: Cover the mixture and refrigerate for at least 1 hour to chill thoroughly. This helps the sorbet freeze more evenly.

4. Churn the Sorbet:

1. **Churn**: Pour the chilled mixture into an ice cream maker and churn according to the manufacturer's instructions, usually about 20-25 minutes, or until it reaches a slushy, sorbet-like consistency.

5. Freeze:

1. **Firm Up**: Transfer the churned sorbet to an airtight container and freeze for at least 2 hours to firm up.

6. Serve:

1. **Scoop and Enjoy**: Scoop the Pomegranate Sorbet into bowls or glasses and enjoy!

Tips:

- **Pomegranate Juice**: If using fresh pomegranates, juice them and strain to remove any seeds or pulp. Store-bought pomegranate juice works well too.
- **Sweetness**: Adjust the sweetness of the sorbet by adding more or less sugar, depending on your taste and the tartness of the pomegranate juice.
- **Ice Cream Maker**: Ensure the ice cream maker's bowl is fully frozen before churning for the best texture.

Enjoy your homemade Pomegranate Sorbet! It's a beautifully tart and sweet frozen dessert that's perfect for any occasion.

Chocolate Covered Strawberry Ice Cream

Ingredients

For the Strawberry Ice Cream Base:

- **2 cups (480ml) whole milk**
- **1 cup (240ml) heavy cream**
- **3/4 cup (150g) granulated sugar**
- **1 cup (240g) fresh strawberries**, hulled and chopped
- **4 large egg yolks**
- **1 teaspoon vanilla extract**

For the Chocolate Swirl:

- **1 cup (175g) semi-sweet chocolate chips** or chopped chocolate
- **1/2 cup (120ml) heavy cream**

Instructions

1. Prepare the Strawberry Ice Cream Base:

1. **Cook Strawberries**: In a medium saucepan, combine the chopped strawberries and granulated sugar. Cook over medium heat, stirring occasionally, until the strawberries are soft and the mixture is thickened, about 10 minutes.
2. **Blend Strawberries**: Transfer the strawberry mixture to a blender or food processor and blend until smooth. Strain through a fine-mesh sieve if you prefer a smoother texture. Let the strawberry puree cool to room temperature.
3. **Heat Milk and Cream**: In a separate saucepan, combine the whole milk and heavy cream. Heat over medium heat until the mixture is hot but not boiling.
4. **Whisk Egg Yolks and Sugar**: In a bowl, whisk the egg yolks and remaining granulated sugar until the mixture is light and slightly thickened.
5. **Temper the Egg Yolks**: Gradually add a small amount of the hot milk mixture to the egg yolks, whisking constantly to temper them.
6. **Cook Custard**: Slowly pour the tempered egg yolks back into the saucepan with the remaining milk mixture. Cook over medium heat, stirring constantly, until the mixture thickens and coats the back of a spoon (170°F-175°F or 77°C-80°C). Do not let it boil.
7. **Combine with Strawberry Puree**: Remove from heat and stir in the strawberry puree and vanilla extract. Mix until well combined. Let the custard cool to room temperature, then cover and refrigerate until very cold (at least 4 hours or overnight).

2. Prepare the Chocolate Swirl:

1. **Heat Cream**: In a small saucepan, heat the heavy cream over medium heat until it begins to simmer.

2. **Melt Chocolate**: Remove from heat and add the chocolate chips. Let sit for a minute, then stir until smooth and fully melted. Let the chocolate mixture cool slightly.

3. Churn the Ice Cream:

1. **Churn**: Pour the chilled strawberry custard into an ice cream maker and churn according to the manufacturer's instructions, usually about 20-25 minutes, or until it reaches a soft-serve consistency.
2. **Add Chocolate Swirl**: During the last few minutes of churning, slowly drizzle in the slightly cooled chocolate mixture to create swirls. You can also fold in the chocolate by hand after churning for larger chunks of chocolate.

4. Freeze:

1. **Firm Up**: Transfer the churned ice cream to an airtight container and freeze for at least 2 hours to firm up.

5. Serve:

1. **Scoop and Enjoy**: Scoop the Chocolate Covered Strawberry Ice Cream into bowls or cones and enjoy!

Tips:

- **Strawberries**: Use ripe, fresh strawberries for the best flavor. You can also use frozen strawberries if fresh ones are not available.
- **Chocolate**: Use high-quality chocolate for the best results. Adjust the amount of chocolate if you prefer more or less swirl.
- **Swirl**: If you prefer a more intense chocolate flavor, you can mix in additional chocolate chunks or swirl more melted chocolate into the ice cream before freezing.

Enjoy your homemade Chocolate Covered Strawberry Ice Cream! It's a delightful blend of fruity sweetness and rich chocolate that's sure to please any palate.

Rhubarb Custard Gelato

Ingredients

For the Rhubarb Purée:

- **2 cups (300g) fresh rhubarb**, chopped
- **1/2 cup (100g) granulated sugar**
- **1/4 cup (60ml) water**

For the Custard Base:

- **2 cups (480ml) whole milk**
- **1 cup (240ml) heavy cream**
- **3/4 cup (150g) granulated sugar**
- **4 large egg yolks**
- **1 teaspoon vanilla extract**

Instructions

1. Prepare the Rhubarb Purée:

1. **Cook Rhubarb**: In a medium saucepan, combine the chopped rhubarb, granulated sugar, and water. Cook over medium heat, stirring occasionally, until the rhubarb is tender and the mixture is thickened, about 10-15 minutes.
2. **Blend Purée**: Transfer the rhubarb mixture to a blender or food processor and blend until smooth. Let the rhubarb purée cool to room temperature.

2. Prepare the Custard Base:

1. **Heat Milk and Cream**: In a medium saucepan, combine the whole milk and heavy cream. Heat over medium heat until the mixture is hot but not boiling.
2. **Whisk Egg Yolks and Sugar**: In a separate bowl, whisk the egg yolks and granulated sugar until the mixture is light and slightly thickened.
3. **Temper the Egg Yolks**: Gradually add a small amount of the hot milk mixture to the egg yolks, whisking constantly to temper them.
4. **Cook Custard**: Slowly pour the tempered egg yolks back into the saucepan with the remaining milk mixture. Cook over medium heat, stirring constantly, until the mixture thickens and coats the back of a spoon (170°F-175°F or 77°C-80°C). Do not let it boil.
5. **Add Vanilla**: Remove from heat and stir in the vanilla extract. Let the custard cool to room temperature, then cover and refrigerate until very cold (at least 4 hours or overnight).

3. Combine Rhubarb Purée and Custard Base:

1. **Mix**: Once the custard base is chilled, fold in the rhubarb purée until well combined.

4. Churn the Gelato:

1. **Churn**: Pour the rhubarb custard mixture into an ice cream maker and churn according to the manufacturer's instructions, usually about 20-25 minutes, or until it reaches a soft-serve consistency.

5. Freeze:

1. **Firm Up**: Transfer the churned gelato to an airtight container and freeze for at least 2 hours to firm up.

6. Serve:

1. **Scoop and Enjoy**: Scoop the Rhubarb Custard Gelato into bowls or cones and enjoy!

Tips:

- **Rhubarb**: If fresh rhubarb is not available, you can use frozen rhubarb. Just thaw and drain excess moisture before cooking.
- **Sweetness**: Adjust the amount of sugar in the rhubarb purée to your taste, especially if you prefer a sweeter gelato.
- **Custard**: Ensure the custard base is fully chilled before mixing with the rhubarb purée for the best texture.

Enjoy your homemade Rhubarb Custard Gelato! It's a creamy and unique frozen treat that pairs the tangy notes of rhubarb with the smooth richness of custard.

Caramel Apple Sorbet

Ingredients

For the Apple Base:

- **4 large apples**, peeled, cored, and chopped (about 4 cups)
- **1 cup (200g) granulated sugar**
- **1/2 cup (120ml) water**
- **1 tablespoon lemon juice** (about 1 lemon)

For the Caramel Swirl:

- **1/2 cup (100g) granulated sugar**
- **2 tablespoons unsalted butter**
- **1/4 cup (60ml) heavy cream**
- **1/4 teaspoon sea salt** (or to taste)

Instructions

1. Prepare the Apple Base:

1. **Cook Apples**: In a medium saucepan, combine the chopped apples, granulated sugar, and water. Cook over medium heat, stirring occasionally, until the apples are tender and the mixture is thickened, about 15-20 minutes.
2. **Blend Apples**: Transfer the cooked apples to a blender or food processor and blend until smooth. You can strain it through a fine-mesh sieve if you prefer a smoother texture. Stir in the lemon juice.
3. **Chill**: Let the apple mixture cool to room temperature, then cover and refrigerate until very cold (at least 2 hours or overnight).

2. Prepare the Caramel Swirl:

1. **Make Caramel**: In a medium saucepan, heat the granulated sugar over medium heat, stirring constantly until it melts and turns a golden amber color. Be careful not to burn it.
2. **Add Butter and Cream**: Once the sugar is fully melted, remove from heat and immediately add the unsalted butter. Stir until the butter is fully incorporated. Slowly add the heavy cream, stirring constantly, until smooth. Be careful as the mixture will bubble up.
3. **Season**: Stir in the sea salt. Let the caramel cool to room temperature.

3. Combine and Churn:

1. **Churn Apple Mixture**: Pour the chilled apple mixture into an ice cream maker and churn according to the manufacturer's instructions, usually about 20-25 minutes, or until it reaches a soft-serve consistency.

2. **Add Caramel Swirl**: During the last few minutes of churning, slowly drizzle in the caramel sauce to create a swirl effect. Alternatively, you can fold the caramel into the sorbet by hand after churning for larger ribbons of caramel.

4. Freeze:

1. **Firm Up**: Transfer the churned sorbet to an airtight container and freeze for at least 2 hours to firm up.

5. Serve:

1. **Scoop and Enjoy**: Scoop the Caramel Apple Sorbet into bowls or glasses and enjoy!

Tips:

- **Apples**: Use tart apples like Granny Smith for a nice balance of sweetness and tartness. You can also mix different apple varieties for a more complex flavor.
- **Caramel**: Make sure to keep a close eye on the caramel as it cooks to avoid burning. If the caramel becomes too thick while cooling, gently reheat it over low heat to loosen it.
- **Ice Cream Maker**: Ensure the ice cream maker's bowl is fully frozen before churning for the best texture.

Enjoy your homemade Caramel Apple Sorbet! It's a delicious and refreshing treat that perfectly combines the flavors of caramel and apple.

Classic Chocolate Ice Cream

Ingredients

- 2 cups (480ml) whole milk
- 1 cup (240ml) heavy cream
- 3/4 cup (150g) granulated sugar
- 1/2 cup (40g) unsweetened cocoa powder
- 4 large egg yolks
- 4 oz (115g) bittersweet or semi-sweet chocolate, chopped
- 1 teaspoon vanilla extract
- 1/4 teaspoon salt

Instructions

1. Prepare the Chocolate Mixture:

1. **Mix Cocoa and Sugar**: In a medium bowl, whisk together the granulated sugar, cocoa powder, and a pinch of salt. Set aside.
2. **Heat Milk and Cream**: In a medium saucepan, combine the whole milk and heavy cream. Heat over medium heat until the mixture is hot but not boiling.
3. **Add Cocoa Mixture**: Gradually whisk the cocoa mixture into the hot milk and cream, and continue to whisk until smooth and well combined. Heat until the mixture is hot, but do not let it boil.
4. **Melt Chocolate**: Remove the saucepan from heat and add the chopped chocolate. Stir until the chocolate is completely melted and the mixture is smooth.

2. Prepare the Custard Base:

1. **Whisk Egg Yolks**: In a separate bowl, whisk the egg yolks until they are light and slightly thickened.
2. **Temper the Egg Yolks**: Gradually add a small amount of the hot chocolate mixture to the egg yolks, whisking constantly to temper them.
3. **Cook Custard**: Slowly pour the tempered egg yolks back into the saucepan with the remaining chocolate mixture. Cook over medium heat, stirring constantly, until the mixture thickens and coats the back of a spoon (170°F-175°F or 77°C-80°C). Do not let it boil.
4. **Add Vanilla**: Remove from heat and stir in the vanilla extract.

3. Chill the Mixture:

1. **Cool**: Let the custard cool to room temperature. Then, cover and refrigerate until very cold, at least 4 hours or overnight.

4. Churn the Ice Cream:

1. **Churn**: Pour the chilled chocolate custard into an ice cream maker and churn according to the manufacturer's instructions, usually about 20-25 minutes, or until it reaches a soft-serve consistency.

5. Freeze:

1. **Firm Up**: Transfer the churned ice cream to an airtight container and freeze for at least 2 hours to firm up.

6. Serve:

1. **Scoop and Enjoy**: Scoop the Classic Chocolate Ice Cream into bowls or cones and enjoy!

Tips:

- **Chocolate**: Use high-quality chocolate for the best flavor. Bittersweet or semi-sweet chocolate will give you a rich chocolate flavor.
- **Cocoa Powder**: Dutch-processed cocoa powder can be used for a smoother, milder chocolate flavor.
- **Ice Cream Maker**: Ensure the ice cream maker's bowl is fully frozen before churning for the best texture.

Enjoy your homemade Classic Chocolate Ice Cream! It's a creamy, indulgent treat that's sure to satisfy any chocolate lover.

Lemon Meringue Gelato

Ingredients

For the Lemon Custard Base:

- 1 cup (240ml) whole milk
- 1 cup (240ml) heavy cream
- 3/4 cup (150g) granulated sugar
- 4 large egg yolks
- 1/2 cup (120ml) fresh lemon juice (about 2 lemons)
- 1 tablespoon lemon zest (about 1 lemon)
- 1 teaspoon vanilla extract

For the Meringue:

- 2 large egg whites
- 1/2 teaspoon cream of tartar
- 1/2 cup (100g) granulated sugar

Instructions

1. Prepare the Lemon Custard Base:

1. **Heat Milk and Cream**: In a medium saucepan, combine the whole milk and heavy cream. Heat over medium heat until the mixture is hot but not boiling.
2. **Whisk Egg Yolks and Sugar**: In a separate bowl, whisk the egg yolks and granulated sugar until the mixture is light and slightly thickened.
3. **Temper the Egg Yolks**: Gradually add a small amount of the hot milk mixture to the egg yolks, whisking constantly to temper them.
4. **Cook Custard**: Slowly pour the tempered egg yolks back into the saucepan with the remaining milk mixture. Cook over medium heat, stirring constantly, until the mixture thickens and coats the back of a spoon (170°F-175°F or 77°C-80°C). Do not let it boil.
5. **Add Lemon**: Remove from heat and stir in the fresh lemon juice, lemon zest, and vanilla extract. Mix until well combined. Let the custard cool to room temperature, then cover and refrigerate until very cold (at least 4 hours or overnight).

2. Prepare the Meringue:

1. **Beat Egg Whites**: In a clean, dry bowl, beat the egg whites with cream of tartar using an electric mixer on medium speed until soft peaks form.
2. **Add Sugar**: Gradually add the granulated sugar, 1 tablespoon at a time, while continuing to beat until stiff, glossy peaks form and the sugar is fully dissolved.
3. **Cool Meringue**: If the meringue is too soft, you can gently fold it into the gelato mixture once the gelato is churned, or use it as a topping when serving.

3. Churn the Gelato:

1. **Churn**: Pour the chilled lemon custard into an ice cream maker and churn according to the manufacturer's instructions, usually about 20-25 minutes, or until it reaches a soft-serve consistency.
2. **Add Meringue**: During the last few minutes of churning, gently fold in spoonfuls of meringue to create swirls. You can also fold the meringue into the gelato by hand after churning for larger pieces.

4. Freeze:

1. **Firm Up**: Transfer the churned gelato to an airtight container and freeze for at least 2 hours to firm up.

5. Serve:

1. **Scoop and Enjoy**: Scoop the Lemon Meringue Gelato into bowls or cones and enjoy!

Tips:

- **Lemon Juice**: Use fresh lemon juice for the best flavor. Bottled lemon juice can have a different taste.
- **Meringue Texture**: If you prefer a more crispy meringue, you can bake the meringue at a low temperature until dried out and then fold in pieces into the gelato.
- **Gelato Maker**: Ensure the ice cream maker's bowl is fully frozen before churning for the best texture.

Enjoy your homemade Lemon Meringue Gelato! It's a delightful frozen dessert that combines the zesty freshness of lemon with the sweet, airy texture of meringue.